Powder

POW

Writing by Women in the Ranks, from Vi

Foreword by Helen Benedict

DER

etnam to Iraq   Edited by Lisa Bowden & Shannon Cain

Kore Press : : Tucson

15.00

Kore Press, Inc.
Tucson, Arizona USA
www.korepress.org

ISBN 13   978-1-888553-25-3

Cover photograph courtesy of Sergeant Sharon D. Allen and Sergeant
Kimberly Archer. Copyright Sharon D. Allen.
Grateful acknowledgment is made to *The Gettysburg Review,* Volume 21, #3,
Autumn 2008, for permission to reprint "Hymn" by Charlotte Brock; and to
Random House, Inc., for "Combat Musician," by Sharon D. Allen, from *Operation
Homecoming,* edited by Andrew Carroll.

FIRST EDITION
Book design by Lisa Bowden

The future will be gorgeous and reckless, and words,
those luminous charms, will set us free again.

—Carole Maso

CONTENTS

CONTRIBUTORS

Foreword

Back when we were only three years into the Iraq war, I went to a veterans' event in New York City to hear soldiers talk about their experiences. There, among all the men in the room, I spotted a young woman standing silently in the back, so I approached her and asked, "Are you a veteran too?"

"Yes, but nobody believes me!" she replied vehemently. "I was in Iraq getting bombed and shot at, but people won't even listen when I say I was at war because I'm a female."

Female soldiers have had trouble being listened to for a long time, even though women have been part of the US military for more than a hundred years. The traditional military attitude towards women has been to regard them as incapable of fighting, so they were neither allowed in battle nor even permitted to carry weapons until after the Vietnam War. This failure to take women soldiers seriously has lasted to this day.

It took the end of the draft, when the Pentagon became desperate for troops, for women's roles in the military to change. Today they make up 14 percent of active duty forces and comprise 11.4 percent of officers serving in the Middle East. As of 2006, more than two thousand women who fought in Iraq or Afghanistan had been awarded Bronze Stars, several for bravery and valor in combat and some thirteen hundred had earned the Combat Action Badge. Women now not only carry weapons but serve in almost all positions in all branches of the military. They only remain banned from submarines and from serving in ground combat divisions such as the infantry. In June of 2008, Lieutenant General Ann E. Dunwoody became the first female four-star general in American history.

In the Iraq war, women soldiers are even more essential. They make up one in ten soldiers, and in spite of the official ban on women in ground combat, they are fighting alongside the infantry and often doing the same jobs as men, partly because of the guerilla nature of the war in Iraq, where there is no real front line, and partly because of the shortage of troops. I have talked to many women who have been gunners atop tanks and trucks, who have raided houses, searched Iraqis, led convoys, who have been shot at, and who have shot others. More women have died and been wounded in Iraq than in the Korean, Vietnam, first Gulf and Afghanistan wars combined.

Yet, in spite of this tremendous change in the role of women soldiers, they are still virtually invisible in the eyes of the American press and public. I have watched at least a dozen documentaries and feature films on the Iraq war, and have read nearly as many books about it, and almost none of them acknowledge the existence of female soldiers. No wonder that young veteran I met said, "Nobody believes me. Nobody listens."

This is why this collection of poetry and prose by women soldiers is so important. It brings the voices of these women to the fore at last, and gives the public a chance to listen. And listen we should, because women tell different war stories than men. They tend to be less in thrall to the masculine posturing that so many military men feel compelled to perpetuate; and they tend to see war and soldierly relations more objectively because it is still so hard for women to be accepted as soldiers at all. As a result, there is little swagger in this collection, but a lot of soul searching.

This is not to say that all the soldiers in this book have similar points of view. Rather, they express a gamut of perspectives on war and the military, some positive, some negative, and some a mix. Christy L. Clothier, a Navy air traffic controller, relates in terrifying detail the night a Navy SEAL tried to rape her. "His right arm secured my shoulder, neck, and chin. I tasted my throat, trapped by a crusty yellowing elbow staring back at me." But she also movingly describes the emotional and physical strength she gained through serving in the military:

"'I wanna hear you scream!' Petty Officer Sampson said on the second day of basic training.' I know you're not here to make Daddy proud! I know you are not here to find a damn man! I know that you have been beaten, hurt, abused! Why else do girls join the military? That's why you have to yell . . . ' Three years earlier, as a military wife, I learned never to yell. Even when my ex-husband tossed my body around the living room by my waist-long hair."

Clothier then tells us she learned not only to yell but to stand up for herself in a way that made her proud. "It was the first time I had heard my voice sound strong." This newfound strength was in part responsible for giving her the wits to outsmart her attacker and escape his attempted rape.

Some of the female soldiers in this book are refreshingly honest about the grueling conditions and moral disgust they experienced at war, especially in Iraq. Others tell of the courage and sacrifices made by their fellow soldiers, and of their pride in their service. Many speak of the divide they feel between their civilian and soldier selves now that they are home. Some write heartbreakingly about the abuse they endured from their supposed comrades. But whatever their tales, and whatever their perspectives, their voices are fresh and important. These women have seen and done things few people ever see or do. They have much to tell us about morality, courage, fear, betrayal and—of course—war.

It is time for us to listen.

—Helen Benedict
Professor of Journalism, Columbia University

Preface

At a writers' conference in Georgia in the summer of 2005, an American veteran of the war in Iraq stood at the podium and read a personal essay about his time as a soldier. Overcome with emotion and using language both beautiful and stark, he told about the mutilations he'd seen, the bloody losses, his struggle with self-hatred upon returning home, and the profound mistrust he now harbored for his commander in chief. The room went silent with respect for his service and horror for his pain.

That day in Georgia, a thought arose: what about the women who have served? Where is *their* perspective? Who will publish *their* words? Thus the idea for this anthology was born.

We put out a call. We asked women in the ranks, especially those who had served after September 11, 2001, to send us their writing. We waited for the flood of responses. Only a few pieces arrived. They were excellent, but not enough to assemble a book-length collection. Then, an email from a soldier who told us of the repercussions, formal and informal, that the military imposes upon those who speak their minds while on active duty.

We reissued our call to military women, farther and wider, and expanded the scope. We asked women who had served anywhere, at any time, to tell their stories. And now the essays and poetry arrived. The writing blew our minds, broke our hearts and gave us hope. And suddenly we found ourselves engaged in a new rendering of American history.

Here was writing that gave us the full scope of the military experience, including a range of ideas about what it means to be a patriot. As advocates for peace and justice, we went into the project with the idea that this book would contribute to the chorus of opposition to the war in Iraq. In the process we found ourselves expanded, and in awe. We saw immediately the necessity of setting aside any bias or agenda. We offer this poetry and this memoir edited but not manipulated, selected but not filtered. In so doing we amplify these voices, and we insist upon their place in a long and nuanced literature of war and peace.

We titled the book *Powder* in recognition of the ways in which women in the ranks live multi-faceted lives, not only as members of the military but also, of course, as mothers, daughters and lovers. We think of gunpowder, baby powder, the powder of rubble. Powdered milk, blasting powder, face powder. The powdery sand of occupied desert countries; the ash that fell on lower Manhattan on September 11. As fans of language we were drawn also to a word that encompasses "power," not to mention "POW."

*

Former Navy Sonar Technician Khadijah Queen understands poetry as "a necessary reaction" to the death of her colleagues. Army Reserve officer Victoria A. Hudson, LTC, who has been mobilized five times in her thirty years of service, says she wrote about what she saw in Bosnia and Iraq in order to "integrate those experiences into memory." Air Force jet engine mechanic K.G. Schneider says she writes to express her gratitude, "so that those who served with me can be remembered."

The writers here are divided on the question of whether they would re-enlist. Marine Corps Officer Charlotte M. Brock has "never regretted joining," but notes "if you asked me that question at various times over the last six years, I would have given a different answer." Former Army Communications Officer Terry Hurley would not hesitate to join again, and is especially drawn to the idea of training new recruits. Arabic linguist Rachel Vigil had "no desire to serve the [Bush] administration's objectives," and says "nothing would talk me into joining again."

Former Air Force medic Deborah Fries looks back at her service during the Vietnam era and realizes if she had it to do over, she "would have marched for peace rather than for a base commander." Bobbi Dykema

Katsanis, who served in the Army National Guard Band, finds the culture of the military "anti-intellectual, sexist, and subliminally violent," and has had to work hard to leave it behind. Former Air Force air traffic controller Christy L. Clothier discovered that the military demanded "silent passivity" and is still in the process of rediscovering her voice. Navy administrative officer Dr. Donna Dean reports she endured "denigration and open hostility throughout her active duty career" and more than 25 years after her discharge still struggles every day with the effects of Post-traumatic Stress Disorder.

But Ohio National Guardsman Sharon D. Allen, who served as a petroleum supply specialist in Iraq and Afghanistan, says that the military gave her a "confidence unrivaled by civilian training." ROTC student Cameron Beattie reports that her experience in Airborne School has changed her forever: "If I can jump out of an airplane, I can do anything." Navy Religious Programs Specialist Dhana-Marie Branton believes she wouldn't be the writer she is today without her military background. "I became myself," she says, "rather than the person others expected me to be. I learned to own my mind."

"The military is a group of diverse human beings like any other," Dykema Katsanis wrote to us in an email. "Some of us are politically liberal or progressive; many of us are against the war and oppose the current administration's foreign policy. Often these voices are squelched in American public discourse."

Regardless of our contributors' divergent views on the war and on the necessity of service, every one of them comes together on one point: it's damn tough to be a woman in the military. Brock, whose essay "Hymn" appears in these pages, says "Why is there no national debate on the fact that women are subject to institutional discrimination in the military? Nowhere else in this country are women so blatantly prohibited from certain jobs solely on the basis of gender. The American public should know what military women have achieved."

*

In the science fiction movie *Contact,* an astronomer/astronaut played by Jodie Foster is launched into space at the invitation of a benign race of extraterrestrial beings. Wide-eyed at what she encounters, she says, "We should have sent a poet."

Indeed we must send poets and writers to places both heavenly and hellish so they can return to describe what the rest of us are incapable of seeing. When we send women to war, they bear witness in ways that men cannot. The memoirists and poets in this volume have stood wide-eyed at the border between war and peace, and in these pages gift us with a record of what they found there.

—L.B. AND S.C.
TUCSON, ARIZONA

I.

WAR DIARY

A record of thoughts and experiences by those in the ranks.

CHARLOTTE M. BROCK

Hymn

I sat outside the hangar on a wood board and sang and prayed. I didn't believe in God, but I opened my mind, my heart, my soul to the universe. I asked for guidance and tried to prepare myself for what I was about to do.

I sat, knees pressed on my chest, and sang what I could remember of three songs over and over. They were my favorites from Mass, which I hadn't attended in years, until I arrived in Camp Victory, Kuwait, in February 2004 and went to a Catholic service out of boredom. By chance, three of the hymns sung in the makeshift chapel that Sunday were my favorites: "Be Not Afraid," "On Eagles' Wings," and "Here I Am, Lord."

A few days later, as I sat in an unarmored HMMWV, facing outboard, ready to take my M-16 off safe and fire at any moment, I watched the Iraqi countryside flashing by . . . *Be not afraid. I go before you always. Come, follow me! And I will give you strength.* I couldn't remember the rest of the words . . . something about not getting hit by flying arrows.

Our convoy made it through all of southern Iraq, up to the Tigris Valley, and west to Anbar Province without getting hit, although the convoy that followed us was attacked. When we stopped for the night at US camps, we could hear the call of the imam from a mosque a few hundred feet away. Getting ready to go to sleep, lying on top of my vehicle, I looked at the stars and felt alive and happy and ready for anything.

Sitting outside the hangar a few weeks later, in Camp Taqaddum, Iraq, on that wood board, I hugged my knees and rocked back and forth for a long time and sang out loud. I was about to do something that I was sure would change me forever. I was in awe of the task at hand. I wanted to be ready. I wanted to know that I was making a conscious choice. I wanted to know that Charlotte, the Charlotte inside the lieutenant, inside the Marine, inside the grown woman, inside the world traveler and the college graduate and the well-lived teen was ready. Beyond experience in the ways of the world and knowledge of heartache and all-knowing cynicism, there was still a Charlotte who was innocent and hopeful and full of love and wonder. The me I imagined was still a little girl. I had to find her and make sure she would be all right through the next few hours.

I sat with my back to the hangar, looking out at the desert. *Here I am, Lord. It is I, Lord.* In the distance, bunkers, hangars, tents. It was late afternoon, and I watched the sky darken. *I have heard you calling in the night!* I tried to remember the rest of the song. I felt the hot air and the board and the sand. I watched the sun and the horizon approach one another. *I will go, Lord, if you lead me.* There was something magical about that song. It seemed to have been written for this moment, for me. *I will hold your people in my heart.*

I came to feel peace. I was calm; time didn't flow like it usually did. The present moment merged with the future times when I knew I would look back on this hour. Everything in my past led up to now, and nothing would be the same after tonight.

Time passed nonetheless, and I got up and went back into the hangar. It was dusk and getting cooler. I had left my surgical blouse inside. I put on a pair of hospital scrubs and waited with the other Marines. Finally we got the call. A team of Marines went to meet the airplane. They came back after about fifteen minutes and parked the truck at the back entrance of the hangar. When I heard them open the door, I turned around and busied myself with putting on rubber gloves, then a facemask. I stared at the equipment on the table in front of me: scissors, pads and ink for fingerprinting, various forms to fill out, pens, bottles of disinfectant, towels, and cleaning gear. I heard steps behind me, slow, hesitant steps from people carrying a heavy, awkward package. They talked through lifting it to the height of the table and putting it down. My back still to them, I heard them unzip the bag. I took a breath, made a final decision—*be not afraid*—and turned around. I was looking at dirty combat boots, then his camouflage pants, and finally his utilities blouse. I forced myself to look at his face. He was dead.

So this was death. So this was a dead body. Simple. Here was a man who was no longer alive. Here was a soldier whose family did not yet know how he would be coming home. Here was a person who had had a life, a story, thoughts, and a consciousness like mine. Here was what everyone I knew—mother, father, sisters—would one day become. Here is how I would end up one day. A body. Gone. Simple.

One Marine was in charge of taking notes and filling out paperwork while another cut off boots, socks, trousers, and shirt as needed to find wounds, tattoos, or other distinguishing marks. It took two of us to take fingerprints of each hand, each finger dipped into ink, pressed onto little boxes on a paper form. We went through the clothes, emptying and inventorying the contents of pockets.

We looked at dog tags. The main job of the Mortuary Affairs unit at Camp Taqaddum was to get tentative ID on all US casualties, and to prepare the remains for shipment to Kuwait, and then to Dover Air Force Base, where DNA samples would be used to positively identify them.

This soldier was not in too bad a state. He had died a few hours before, from gunshot wounds, and rigor mortis had already set in. His body, although dirty, stiff, and pale, was intact. His mouth was set in a rictus, which made him difficult to look at for too long. The smell was wet and sweet and thick. He was there. My position in the huge room was relative to him. He was the zero around which we moved, quietly but quickly. Even as I was there, and fully engaged in the work at hand, I could see myself looking back and regarding the scene from above. As he was seeing it?

You who dwell in His shadow for life . . .

As I worked more bodies over the next weeks and months, I came to sense, or imagine, or imagine I was sensing, them looking at us, at me. *And He will raise you up on eagles' wings . . .* Floating somewhere among the rafters of the hangar, they took note of what we were doing. They observed as we carried in the body bags from the back door, set them on the operating tables, and unzipped them. They saw what they looked like dead, and watched to see how we, the ones still alive, reacted. I could not grimace or turn my head in disgust. They might see it and feel sorry for themselves, or for me.

Bear you on the breath of dawn. Here were bodies of men whom their loved ones would cry over and want to hold and cherish and love.

The mothers and wives of these fallen angels were present in some way to me, in addition to the men themselves: the souls of the dead and their survivors looking down and observing us.

They couldn't act or touch or talk, but I could. I could take care of them as if they were babies. I could look at their faces and see that they were individuals, and unique, and beautiful. *Make you to shine like the sun!* I could find something to love about them. *And hold you in the palm of His hand.*

In the weeks that followed my first Mortuary Affairs experience, an image kept flashing in my mind, a memory or a symbol that I couldn't quite identify. It had to do with me at the table, bent over the angel lying before me. Seeing myself there reminded me of something, but I couldn't say what. Had I seen this in a dream? Read it in a book? It was something more universal, something timeless yet deeply tied to me and my memories.

When a call came in that angels were incoming, I would feel dread . . . but also adrenaline and anticipation. *Here I am, Lord. Is it I, Lord?* I wanted to be there when they came. *I have heard you calling in the dark.* I wanted to take care of them. I had to; nobody could do it as well I could. *I will go, Lord, if you lead me.* Nobody was as conscious of them as someone's baby as I was. No one would touch them as gently and look at them as lovingly as I would. *I will hold your people in my heart.* I was never as conscious of life and of my soul as when I was waiting for their arrival.

There were times when I wanted to kiss them. My hands lingered on them longer than was necessary. I didn't want to be the note taker; I wanted to handle the bodies themselves. I would reach across the table, grab a shoulder or a hip, and pull it into my body, to allow the Marine on the other side to get a look at the back. I pulled IVs out of their veins as gently as I could; I knew it was crazy, but I didn't want to hurt them. I cut off socks and looked at dead feet and toes. I saw holes in every part of their bodies. I saw bones sticking out of flesh. I saw brains leaking out from heads and eyes that had been popped out of sockets. Bodily fluids dripped on my boots. I gagged at horrid smells. I jumped back when the swollen, bright red body of a drowned man belched up water and weeds.

I opened a bag whose contents bore no semblance to the shape of a man. We found a head. An arm with a hand. And a hand. The rest consisted of torn rags of a uniform, gore and intestines and slabs of skin covered in shit and blood. The head was perfect, serene. I closed his gray eyes. He had a beautiful face with fine, perfect features and a small, distinctive moustache. He was a gunnery sergeant, and he wore a ring on the fourth finger of each hand. We spread him out over three tables to try to figure him out. I put his hand in mine and took it over to a table, then got his arm, torn off above the elbow. I fingerprinted him. It was much easier to get each finger at the right angle, as there was no body attached. We identified what we could and tried to put him back in the bag in some kind of order, but all we could do was place his head where his head should be and his hands on either side. We put the rest in the middle.

Half a dozen sailors were killed at once by indirect fire. They had been playing soccer at their camp on a Sunday morning. Their bodies occupied all the tables in the hangar. Another time, some Civil Affairs soldiers were hit by an IED hidden in a tree. They had been going to a village to distribute supplies to a school. Their lieutenant was not hurt. He came to see them at Mortuary Affairs. Here was a young man, my age, who had just lost four of his soldiers. Here was someone who would have to speak to their parents and live the rest of his life with this burden. And here I was, me, Charlotte, who had to talk to him. And say what? How do you offer comfort to a stranger? How do you avoid banalities and platitudes but still say something you mean? He asked if he could have his soldiers' dog tags. We couldn't give them to him. But I got a piece of paper and a pencil and got the imprint of his soldiers' tags for him. I was so happy to give him something. I was proud of myself for thinking of doing this.

Time spent in Mortuary Affairs was time spent in a world apart. Nothing mattered like taking care of the people who came to us. This place became the center, the core, of my existence. It was what gave meaning, significance, to my life. I was a caretaker, a love giver, the mother of the dead. I was Mary bringing Jesus down from the cross and washing her son's body before laying it in the grave. I was the eternal feminine holding the body of the fallen warrior, who in death is just a little boy.

Three years later I still don't know how, or how well, or whether, I have dealt with the entire deployment. I know I have changed in some ways. I learned to love life more. I became more emotional. I now see beauty where I never saw it before. But part of me is still there. Part of me wishes I was still with them. Part of me feels that is where I should be: wiping away the blood and grime from a young man's face so that his fellow soldier can come tell us, "Yes, it's him."

RACHEL VIGIL

Commander in Chief

As you know, these are open forums,
you're able to come
and listen to what I have to say. *

1.
around the world there's been
tremendous death and destruction
because killers kill
free societies will be allies
against these hateful few
who have no conscience,
who kill at the whim of a hat.

2.
I'm honored to shake the hand
of a brave Iraqi citizen
who had his hand cut off by Saddam Hussein
and, you know, it'll take time
to restore chaos and order—
but we will. See,
free nations are peaceful nations
free nations don't attack each other
free nations don't develop
weapons of mass destruction.
I went to the Congress last September
and proposed fundamental—supplemental funding
which is money for armor and body parts
and ammunition and fuel
we've got hundreds of sites to exploit

you see, not only did the attacks
help accelerate a recession,
the attacks reminded us that we are at war
obviously, I pray every day
there's less casualty.

3.
it's the birds that's supposed to suffer, not the hunter
see, in my line of work
you got to keep repeating things
over and over and over again for the truth to sink in,
to kind of catapult the propaganda.
in this job you've got a lot
on your plate on a regular basis;
you don't have much time to sit
around and wander, lonely,
in the Oval Office, kind of asking
different portraits, how do you think my standing will be?

you know, I don't spend a lot of time thinking
about myself, about why I do things.
I always jest to people;
the Oval Office is the kind of place
where people stand outside,
they're getting ready to come in and give
me what for, and they walk in and get
overwhelmed by the atmosphere.
and they say, man you're looking pretty.

*(All of the above are the unaltered quotations of
President George W. Bush between 2003 and 2005.)*

RACHEL VIGIL

Gear Up

weight: *276 lbs*

Shoulders
M16 A-2's (2)
with chamber plugs (2)
bag for night vision goggles (1)
with NVG's inside (1)
head harness (1)
AA batteries (4)
bags of jelly beans (2)
GPS system (1)

Waist and left thigh
gas mask carrier (1)
gas mask turned inside-out (1)
charcoal decontamination packs (2)
atropine injections (2)
field journal (1)
and pen (1)
orange (1)
power bar (1)
English-Arabic Dictionary (1)

Head
kevlar helmet
cammo cover (1)
Witness Locator Card (1)
(information already filled out)
Casualty Feeder Card (1)
(information already filled out)

in ziplock baggie
under kevlar lining
camouflage bandana (1)
goggles (1)
(strapped around Kevlar)
I.D. tags (2) *(on neck chain)*
(checked 4 times)

Left breast
embroidered name tag
dad wore in '73 (1)

Chest
black pen (1)
military I.D. (1)
(checked 4 times)
Arabic visa
military driver's license (1)
wallet (1)
with I.D.
(checked 4 times)
credit cards
civilian passport
photo wrapped in plastic (1)
earplug case (1)
hanging from buttonhole
with 1″ red laser flashlight (1)
notepad
Social Security Numbers (8)
(last 4 digits yelled out loud)
weapons serial numbers (8)
(checked 4 times)
of all your soldiers
weather and percent-illumination data

Shoulders and chest
Load-Bearing Equipment Vest (1)

full canteens (2)
coffee packets (2)
tissue pack (1)
power bars (2)
in magazine compartments
tiny chessboard (1)
in grenade cup
X-large rucksack with frame (1)
2-gallon ziplock (1)
with full set of Desert Camouflage Uniform (1)
socks (2)
bra (1)
pair underwear (1)
brown t-shirt (1)
small ziplocks (3)
each holding
socks (2)
underwear (1)
bra (1)
brown t-shirt (1)
hygiene bag (1)
chapstick (1)
shampoo (1)
dial (1)
boxed tampons (3)
hair rubber bands (5)
comb (1)
aspirin (1)
sleeping pills (1)
Tums (1)
small towel (1)
large pack of baby wipes (1)
sunflower seeds (1)
single-serving laundry soap (2)
CD player (1)
and CDs (20)
deck of Chippendale's playing cards (1)

empty 30-round M-16 magazines (4)
550-cord (350')
and clothespins (7)
comfy boots (2)
a field-stripped MRE (1)

Left leg
bolts to M-16 rifles (9)
keychain (1)
with compass (1)
thermometer (1)
Leatherman (1)

Right leg
ziplock baggies
with baby wipes (2)
stridex pads (1)
Chapstick (1)
tampons (4)
pack Kleenex (1)
calling card (1)
phone numbers (5)

Duffel bag
(on top of rucksack)
packed in order of use
sleeping mat
flak vest (1)
in bottom
Nuclear Biological Chemical MOPP suit (1)
decontamination kit (1)
rubber boots (1)
rubber gloves (2)
in MOPP sack (1)
full sets of DCU's (4)
each in 2-gallon ziplocks
packs of baby wipes (2)

small ziplocks (10)
with socks (2)
underwear (1)
bra (1)
brown t-shirt (1)
ziplock with P.T. suit (1)
white socks (2)
running shoes (2)
gore-tex jacket (1)
and pants (1)
poncho (1)
(with a length of 550-cord
tied to each corner eyelet for shade)
towel in a ziplock (1)
sleeping bag (1)
extra lock (1).
blue tape
(unit colors)
around the bag.
name
and unit tag
on handle.

SHARON D. ALLEN

Combat Musician

Most of my platoon is comprised of guys who work as prison guards in the civilian world. One of my best friends here is Shannon Bear, a 240-pound, six-foot three-inch prison guard. When he got back from leave, he brought with him a new toy.

A fiddle.

In the middle of Iraq, Bear's learning to play the fiddle. He's really, really happy because he's almost got two songs down. "Mary Had a Little Lamb" and "Twinkle, Twinkle Little Star." You have to picture this grown man all excited because, as he said, he's "almost ready to turn the page!"

To "Little Brown Jug."

If you can't beat 'em, join 'em, so now I'm trying to pick it up. Got "Mary Had a Little Lamb" and "Twinkle, Twinkle Little Star" and a start at "Camptown Races." I am notorious for my lack of patience, however, so I convinced Bear to jump ahead to "Amazing Grace," which was in chapter twenty-six. Keep in mind, we were on chapter four.

He got the first two notes right off the bat, and we were really impressed with ourselves until we realized that we could not read sheet music.

"What's that little slashy-thingy?" I asked. "If we could figure out what that is, I can get it." Oh, yes, with the fiddle, as with most things, a little bit of knowledge is a dangerous thing.

Later we found a book with "Amazing Grace" without the little slashy-thingies. We are now unstoppable.

SHARON D. ALLEN

Lost in Translation

We work with a lot of Turks and Iraqis, especially Kurds. I wish that every deployed soldier had a chance to meet them because they are very different from the Arabs to the south. The Kurds love us.

I started to learn Kurdish to keep score in volleyball. Eventually I learned about two hundred words and phrases, but it wasn't so easy because they have sounds Americans can't pronounce. They can't say "left" or "six" for some reason, so I guess we're even.

One of our guys brought this guitar around to the guard shacks and played some American music for them. Note to Enrique Iglesias: Iraqis know you. For what it's worth, you rank right up there with Michael Jackson, Madonna, and Shakira.

Sometimes they'd try to join in. You haven't lived until you've seen a bunch of Iraqi soldiers, complete with AK-47s, sitting around and singing with gusto as they mangle the Beatles'"Let It Be."

In times of trouble, mother Mary comes to me, speaking words of wisdom . . . Little Pea."

They really got into it.

Little Pea, Little PEA! Little Pea, yeah, Little Pea . . . Whisper words of wisdom, Little Pea.

It was a good day.

II.

PAYING DUES

Proving one's dedication; a term of respect for a colleague's commitment and endurance.

K. G. SCHNEIDER

Falling In

"I tell ya, I'd do it in a heartbeat," said Donna. She was sitting on the edge of her cot, sprucing up the display drawer in her locker with a piece of scotch tape wrapped around two fingers, delicately lifting up dots of dust that might earn her demerits if Sergeant Strale caught them on morning inspection. I was spraddled on the cool linoleum floor of the training barracks, buffing my shoes to a high-gloss shine with a length of pantyhose wrapped around my hand. The room stank of shoe leather and cologne.

Erin rolled her eyes and whispered to the ceiling, "Everything the TI say, Donna gotta say."

That morning, Sergeant Strale, our Training Instructor, had been riffing on his military exploits as we, the two dozen recruits in his training squadron, stumbled across a parade ground in one of our first marching formations at this Air Force training camp in Texas. It was ten hundred hours, as we were learning to say, and hot as a pistol. We had been marching off and on since Reveille had sounded at oh four hundred.

"Oh yeah, Italy, I'd go there again in a heartbeat," Sergeant Strale claimed as we grimly clattered across the asphalt, the humidity softening the creases in our new uniforms. "But y'all gotta sweep under your car with a mirror every morning, checking for bombs. I'm serious as a heart attack. *Oh* yeah. I'm serious as an open grave. Those terrorists, they'll blow you out of the sky."

It was 1983. In Italy, terrorists had, in fact, attacked American military bases. As Sergeant Strale spoke, I'd tripped, distracted by the sudden image of an open grave with me tumbling into it. My wobbling caused a ripple in our formation and we hewed left and right before cleaving back to formation.

"Jesus, ladies, get it together," said Sergeant Strale. "Learn yer leff-right-leff."

We had arrived at Lackland several days earlier and had been desperately trying to "get it together" ever since. As I stumbled off the bus a voice had shouted "Fall in!" *Fall in what?* I thought. My lungs labored to pull in the wet, furnace-hot air of an August day in Texas, and my head swirled from too much happening at once: barking TIs, rumbling buses, and the glaring afternoon sun. Standing in formation in front of the rumbling bus, shivering with fear and excitement, I felt myself wanting to fall in to military life, to position myself on this map.

One TI paced back and forth in front of our formation. "So, you miss your mommies?"

I wanted to laugh—this scene was right out of a B movie—but my stomach fluttered, and a thin, sour bile bubbled at the back of my throat. We were standing at half-assed attention, unsure what to do with our arms or hands, our tennis shoes sinking into the heat-softened asphalt. Hordes of other recruits jolted and jerked around us. *Do not mention missing family,* I scribbled on my mental notepad.

Tears slid down one recruit's face, striping her cheeks with dusky black mascara. I tried to ignore her, but I felt my own eyes sting and my throat grow thick with grief, and without looking left or right knew I would soon be amidst a female epidemic of weeping. I, for one, did miss my mommy right then, even though I was 26 years old, only visited my mother once or twice a year, and often forgot her birthday. More to the point, I missed civilian life, which just yesterday had seemed so boring and dead-end, but now, as my knees trembled and my body dampened and prickled with flop-sweat, was already tinted with sepia-toned nostalgia.

"Oh, for Christ's sake, don't cry," bellowed another TI, a tall, barrel-chested sergeant with proud duck-lips and an ageless forehead, over which the rim of a ranger hat waggled as he ranted and scolded. This, it would turn out, was Sergeant Strale, our squadron's TI for the next six weeks. "Come on, ladies, get it TOGETHER! Suck it up!"

Suck it up? The crying recruit hiccupped and sniffled, then became quiet. Two dozen brains processed this expression, which in 1983 was still largely heard only in military circles.

Soon, with Sergeant Strale's help, I would learn that "suck" is a canonical military verb, one even more pervasive than "fuck," the all-purpose verb, noun, prefix, and suffix that, though it put the F in FUBAR, could not be uttered In Front of Officers. But at that moment, as I mulled over these new words, someone screamed "Forward harch," and we lurched forward into our experience, not at all sure what a harch was but desperate to do well at it.

The first two days at Lackland we were "harched" through green building after green building in a supersonic, amped-up version of the "inprocessing" I would repeat at five duty stations in my Air Force career. Doctors poked and squinted at us to verify that the recruiters had delivered healthy goods, nurses jabbed us with vaccination needles, and expressionless airmen—not trainees, but the real thing, with stripes on their sleeves—handed us paperwork thick with inky carbon paper that turned our hands blue.

Words whizzed past me rapid-fire. *Ten hut forward harch big time terrectly get on over here chow duffle parade rest order arms. Your leff. Your leff. Damn it, airman, your military leff!* I was like a game-show contestant caroming through a grocery store, stuffing vocabulary willy-nilly in my cart. *Watch your cover:* in formation, stand directly behind the person in front of you. *Scrambled eggs:* the gold braid senior officers wore on their uniforms. *Buddy system:* don't go anywhere alone.

In childhood, words were my citadel. I read early and precociously, not for ideas or setting or character, but for the taste and feel of words in my mouth. I read *Treasure Island* for the pirate language: scuppers and spyglasses and yo-ho-ho, and fifteen men so small they could stand on a dead man's chest. I read Thurber for his wacky urbanities, and made arch references I hardly understood to "the high-water mark of my youth," the phrase that opens Thurber's essay "The Night the Bed Fell." I read British murder mysteries for their tea-cozy aphorisms; I read *Consumer Reports* for the words that accompanied its descriptions of household appliances that exploded or cars that flipped over. Words mesmerized and comforted me, and the fortress of language allowed me to forget for a bit what it was like to be short, fat, pimply, slow on the playground, and a sniveler, with hair as wiry as the braces on my teeth.

As I grew older, the pimples faded but the awkwardness did not, and I built that wall of words thicker and higher. For much of the previous decade I had lived in the world of an English major, laconically attending college on the eight-year plan. I had no real skills, very little discipline, and a work history that couldn't get me a job selling shoes. Until my enlistment, my world had been defined by grand and largely unproven theories, such as *get accepted into law school and your family will love you,* or *it's hard to get evicted in New York City.*

No one who knew me predicted I would get through Basic Training, and I wasn't too sure myself. But I made one decision in college that may have foreshadowed my survival in the military: when it became apparent that deconstruction was the current vogue for literary theory, I backed away from my hazy plan to pursue graduate studies in English. Jane Austen's Emma Woodhouse, in her officious and amusing grandeur, was far more real to me than Derrida's theories. I can see Emma pouting at Sergeant Strale and scheming to get out of our morning runs. Emma, I believe, would have enjoyed the challenge of Basic Training and would have made the other ladies laugh. Emma would have loved shooting an M-16.

On Day 3, after we ran, marched, ate, marched some more, and after Sergeant Strale scolded us for being the worst marchers "Lackland has evah seen—*evah,*" we were herded into yet another anonymous green cinderblock building and guided toward long tables piled with uniforms. Civilians in hairnets eyed us once over, then handed us stacks of clothes and shoes that would turn out to fit us, more or less. Other faceless civilians then sewed name tags on our shirts, and with our uniforms tucked under our left arms (so our right arms were free for saluting) we marched back to our barracks, for the first time silent not with fear but excitement.

"Double-time-it, ladies, we hain't got all day. And watch your gig lines," shouted Sergeant Strale. The gig line is the alignment of the shirt placket with the pants placket, and you are in excellent company if you have never paid attention to this sartorial detail. I still check it automatically after I dress, running my thumb from neck to bellybutton in one swift motion.

After yanking on our new clothes, we twisted and turned in front of the full-length mirrors in the barracks bathroom, staring at ourselves with disbelief and pride. Our hair was pixie-short or pinned neatly above our collars and ears; our shirts sported our names above our left pockets; our feet were clad in the coal-black oxfords known as low quarters. (Later, on active duty, many of us would wear jungle boots, well-liked foot-friendly black leather boots with green weave inserts around the ankles; I took mine out of the box in the garage last night, and they were still pristinely, proudly shined.) We tried on our covers—hats—though wearing them indoors was forbidden, just as covers were worn outdoors at all times except when working on or around airplanes. I even exulted over the military-issue eyewear required in Basic Training: heavy black corrective spectacles so excruciatingly ugly they were known as BCGs: Birth Control Glasses. We folded away our civvies and with them our former lives.

We were all there to start over. We came from east, west, north, and south, city and country and suburb and exurb, dragging our cheap suitcases and our dreams of a better life. We brought our own languages with their own special meanings, tucked in with our address books and rabbits' feet and dog-eared photographs of our last family gatherings. We had grown up where soda was pop or Pepsi or cola, or where a big sandwich was a hero or a hoagie or a grinder, or where hello was hi or hey-yah or hullo or howdy or hey. But we didn't want those languages any more. We ached to be part of this new world, a land leagues from the dead-end pink-collar jobs or the dull men down the street our parents wanted us to marry or the gang drive-bys or the Saturdays spent wandering around suburban shopping malls, fingering things we could not afford, or the nights spent channel-surfing in the living room of a home snowfall-quiet after the death of a child. And so we tiptoed out the door, past the father (brother, mother, sister) slumped at the kitchen table, drunk by noon, past the photo of the grinning fiancé found nailing our best friend after the party, past the stench of youthful disappointment.

Sometimes our old lives had nothing wrong with them except we just didn't want to be in them, as if even at our young age we understood the short calendar of human existence. *Know what I mean?* we whispered into the night, staring up into the darkness from our cots, trying not to move so our uniforms would still be crisp in the morning. *I know. Me too. Cain't really 'splain it.* So we blinked back tears and mouthed the new words, adopting our new mother tongue.

In the barracks that fourth afternoon, Donna sighed deeply as she tilted her head, looking for more dust specks. Her low quarters sparkled under the fluorescent lights, and I buffed mine a little harder.

"Yeah," she said, "we gotta get it together. Big-time. I'm serious as a heart attack. I'm serious as an open grave."

This time all of us sprawled on the barracks floor rolled our eyes, but not without admiration. Donna was Sergeant Strale's amanuensis, the first to repeat his words onto our collective slate. *In a heartbeat. Serious as a heart attack. Serious as an open grave.* These new phrases rippled through our ranks as we straightened the barracks and obsessively inspected and re-inspected our new uniforms, as we tumbled down the concrete stairs of the barracks and fell into formation, as we marched to and from the chow hall. All day and into the evening we passed Sergeant Strale's phrases among us like dope smokers sharing a bong. We polished shoes, worked on our cots' hospital corners, dabbed paint on belt buckles to keep them evenly black, or folded and refolded t-shirts, holding a straight-edge ruler against the edges. We had to line up for meals, not just quickly, but in a heartbeat. *In a heartbeat.* We were all serious as a heart attack. Heart attack. If we didn't stand at attention we were going to get it *"big-time, oh, yeah." Big time. Oh, yeah. In a heartbeat. Heart attack. Big time.*

Most days, when we were not running, marching, or trying to stay awake in darkened auditoriums as sergeants lectured us about customs and courtesies, personal hygiene, or the history of the Air Force, Sergeant Strale held forth in our barracks.

"Ladies!" Sergeant Strale would boom, pacing back and forth in front of a tall wooden podium as we sat cross-legged before him, two dozen acolytes at the Adoration of the TI. "We don't talk like jarheads, or squids, or grunts!"—to whom we were to refer, In Front Of Officers, as marines, seamen, and soldiers. "We are AIRMEN!" roared Sergeant Strale, his backswept hair slipping not one lock over his patriotic forehead. My flesh raced with a proprietary thrill. I was someone; I was an airman. I looked around. Even Robin, the practical earth-mother from one of those square states in the center of the country, was staring at Sergeant Strale, lips parted, as if she wanted to bear his children. It was immaterial that we were not men, but two dozen women: quibbling over sexist language was the sort of hair-splitting you'd expect from weak-sister civilians with their lazy liberal ways.

"You don't wanna be an airman no more, get yerselves promoted to SERGEANT!" shouted Sergeant Strale. On reflection, this was practical, empowering advice. Only in the previous ten years had the armed forces lifted the ceiling on women in the military (formerly limited to two percent of the corps), equalized men's and women's salaries, opened hundreds of closed specialties, and made promotion to higher ranks a reality. Sergeant Strale had enlisted in the days when women were recruited for their typing skills, made to wear skirts and heels, and were expected to marry officers and leave the military. Still, he was quite the feminist. His ambitions for us, when we had done well, were no less than swift advancement to "Chief Master Sergeant of the whole entire YEW ESS AY EFF!"

Not all advice was empowering, even when it was practical. "Schneider, you don't get it together, yer ass gonna be on rollerskates, right outta Lackland," screamed Sergeant Santera, Sergeant Strale's assistant. I was on the cement apron in front of our barracks, and I had marched right instead of left, or perhaps I had wussed out before the end of our morning run and collapsed panting on the cinder track, or maybe I had fallen into formation half a second late. It is hard to remember; there were so many transgressions.

Sergeant Santera was two inches taller than me, so when she tipped her head forward and screamed, my eyes were level with the crown of her ranger hat, which bobbed and tilted in front of me like an asp angling for a strike. Though my armpits were gushing and I was praying for an earthquake or nuclear attack to release me from this misery, I could not help noticing that Sergeant Santera's diction was impeccable. The "don't" like "dohn" and the "gonna" very nearly one syllable. Her inflection rose and fell as if it were itself on rollerskates, gliding around a rink of TI Haiku, a bit of craft with irregular metrics and feminine endings:

> *The Screaming*
>
> You don' get it toGETHer
> Yer ass gon' be on ROLLerskates
> Right outta LACKland
>
> — Sergeant Santera, Lackland AFB, August, 1983

I, a desperate understudy trembling in my fatigues and BCGs, listened carefully, if not to the meaning of what Sergeant Santera was saying—mostly, she was telling me I was clumsy, slow-moving, and disorganized, a message that rarely changed, and was unfortunately true—then to the alluring way she said it, in honeyed, elegant Air Force English.

I learned quite a bit from Sergeant Santera, whether she was screaming at me or, in one of her better moods, leaning against the TI's podium in the barracks, thumping one lacquered low-quarter on the shining linoleum while she taught us the unvarnished dactyls and anapests that would serve us so well: *Hell and back. Kiss my ass. Give it up. Holy Joe*—which was a chaplain, and also a large perforated envelope used to move paper between offices.

Seated on the barracks floor, we absorbed our catechism, soaking up a language flavored by its origins in the Army Air Corps, which in turn can trace its Army heritage back to the Revolutionary War and beyond. It is Southern-influenced, quasi-grammatical, colorful, and strong, short on egghead words and sissy-la-la lingo. Nobody "processes feelings" in the Air Force.

Two weeks into training, my Air Force English was still bad. My accent, which I had deliberately allowed New York to cultivate, so that dog was *dwahg* and coffee became *kwahfee,* now cruelly revealed my Yankee ways. My book-built vocabulary branded me as an overeducated outsider. My nuances spoke to the weasely, prevaricating, quibbling world I had come from. I pushed myself to replace "but" with "yes, sir." Even a word such as *cleanse,* when everyone else said clean, was a damned spot I needed to out. Literary allusions, polysyllabic *bon mots,* or quotations: bad, bad, bad. Mostly, I kept my mouth shut and listened to the lexicon buzzing around my head.

Some of our education came from worldlier recruits, classes several weeks ahead of us, a whispered schooling behind dumpsters or in latrines or mumbled troop to troop while we stood in formation on a griddle-hot parade ground. From our peers we learned coarser, less interesting iambics: *Eat shit and die. Go fuck yourself. Nuke 'em 'til they glow. Blow 'em out of the water.*

I was gradually adjusting to the reality of military life, which in the abstract seemed dashing and noble but, like most of life's activities, proved up close to have considerable quotidian drabness. I did like my brave new world far more than the civilian life I had left, with its chaos and discouragements. I liked the promise of difference, the way the new life enveloped me in strange practices, clothing, and language. I liked the hoarse-voiced young women in my squadron, resilient and clever humans who had pulled themselves up out of drab rust-belt towns and chaotic ghettos and crumbling frame houses along country roads, women who like me had bucked the tide that in 1983 still said women couldn't run away to join the military.

Women like me. I was surprised and delighted and ashamed to see how these women draped themselves in this new language as eagerly as I did, moving their teeth and tongues over these new words, chanting and incanting. As ignorant as Emma Woodhouse, I had believed that love of the language was an art cultivated in higher education, not a gift shared by so many of our species. Now I lay in the dark at night and listened to the sibilant accents of Georgia and Alabama and Ohio, heard the slow giggles of a Kentucky gal, and marveled how in their speech they had so quickly adopted our new signifiers, drawling them out in beauty. *In a heartbeat. I'll get on it terrectly. Thirty-nine days and a wake-up.* Their voices were so many crickets, chirruping softly as I fell asleep, a murmuring wall of sound.

By week 4, after I had passed the confidence course, shot a gun, and made it around the track without collapsing short of breath, my language skills were beginning to fall in step. Leave off the egghead terms. Start some sentences with "say." Throw in *do believe* and *terrectly* and *you-all* now and then. Don't lay it on too thick.

"Say, Karen, you got some Kiwi shoe polish leff?"

"Say, I do believe so. I'll dig it up terrectly."

It was a lingua franca at once concrete and metaphorical, specific and universal. Air Force words, resembling Air Force life itself, were crunchy, chewy entities, steeped in pungent sensory impressions, liquid with Southern vowels, or bright with hard bomb-dropping consonants. In those barracks, seven years before I would travel to Korea, I learned you didn't want to be in *deep kimchee*. Nowhere in the Air Force, for my entire career, did you want to be caught *quibbling:* the pragmatic, action-focused military couldn't bear such *wussy* behavior.

But balance is everything. It was also wrong to be *ate up* or *gung-ho:* over-enthusiastic about military service. "She so ate up, she like to give them back her birthday," giggled Erin one afternoon late in our training, as we stood sweltering on the Lackland parade grounds, stepping through remedial marching drills assigned for some collective offense. It was just after Labor Day. The air smelled of faded summer dust, and my feet, in their nylon socks, slithered hot and wet in my low quarters. The recruit in question, aside from saluting everything in sight, had that morning insisted on being the first to walk into a trailer filled with teargas, where we were being taught to don gas masks in under ten seconds.

Over the next eight years I would frequently hear variations on this expression. "What're they gonna do, take away my birthday?" we asked in times of duress. The Air Force could pull stripes, dock pay, send you to a remote tour at the end of hell, or even toss you out with a bad-conduct discharge, but your birthday they could not touch.

By now I dined on *chow* in the *mess hall,* cleaned up rooms by *policing* them, slept on a *rack,* and—in a dainty reversion to an earlier era—no longer wore underpants but *underthings,* a term that evoked petticoats and other clothes far frillier than the plain white cotton garments we could buy at the *BX.* That suspicious-looking "butter" in the mess hall was universally called *oleo.*

If Sergeant Strale was our lexicographer and chief linguist, Sergeant Santera served as our muse, our strategist, and, in her grumpy manner, our champion. As the weeks progressed, she shouted us over climbing walls and taught us how to crawl in a trench, screaming "Get yer butts lower, ladies!" Grinning, she chunked pebbles at our bottoms.

I sucked it up, tried again and again, and sometimes earned a tip of her ranger hat. She taught us how to march *eyes right,* our faces turned toward the review stand, our right hands angled at crisp salutes, while our feet maintained a perfectly syncopated leff-right-leff. As she marched alongside us, her stentorian voice pulling us forward, her ranger hat perfectly level with the ground at all times, she also taught us cadence, that mellifluous marching music set to firm trochees in a foot-stomping catalectic that I describe here in its cleanest form:

> I don't know but I've been told
> Air Force wings are made of gold

> I don't know but it's been said
> Army wings are made of lead

"Sound off, one two," we cried, marching forward into military life in our crisp fatigues, utterly satisfied with our drill. We knew our *right flank* from our *parade rest,* our *forward harch* from our *prepare to execute;* we were a clockwork formation of feminine warriors moving in precision across the parade grounds, arms and legs confidently scissoring above the asphalt. "Sound off, three four. One, two, three, four. One, two, THREE FOUR!"

"We gotta pass that running test next week. I'm serious as an open grave," I whispered to Erin.

"Serious as a heart attack," she agreed.

"Roger that," I concluded, and felt a flash of gladness.

By our sixth week, when we would graduate, Air Force language was a sheath of protective words as warm and snug as the quilted liner I would button into my regulation parka that first winter, thousands of miles from Texas. Gradually, I attuned myself to military life and the sounds and voices that typified it, and my New York accent faded. Though my accent never became Southern, my spoken voice blended into a less definable pastiche that served me well across five tours on four continents over eight years, a pleasant mutt accent that trotted after me into civilian life. *Where are you from?* people ask, even today. *All over,* I reply. *All over.*

BOBBI DYKEMA KATSANIS

Fort Dix, 1989

drill sergeants nose to nose and screaming insults
bootheels crunching in the gravel,
snarling mocking barking orders.

that summer in New Jersey,
as the sand ground into open, weeping blisters
on my heels,
mosquito bites flared red as beacons,
my dreams were filled with shouting.
body-sore and aching,
sleeping under scratchy green wool blankets,
or out in the dark woods,
the smell of burning carbon sharp in my nostrils.

morning dawned,
I looked up and saw an airplane, a C-130
soaring west.
I wished that I was on it,
didn't care where it was going.

CAMERON BEATTIE

Leaping to Earth

I jumped out of an airplane for the first time last summer. I leaned my body over the edge of the platform, hands locked on either side of my reserve parachute, ready to go. Far below, the landscape passed slowly. The earth looked like a model made of felt and pipe cleaners. Then the trees ran out, replaced by smooth yellows and greens.

The jumpmaster grabbed my pack, pulling me back into the plane.

"Not yet, Airborne!" he yelled over the wind. In a moment, the green light to my left would light up and I would receive a firm slap on the right buttock. I would leap, falling 500 feet as the plane hurtled away. I would sway, alone. The landing site—dry grass and earth, caked hard by the landings of parachutists—would rush closer and closer.

Every morning in airborne school, the jumpmaster stood on a platform facing 364 men and women from different countries, backgrounds and branches of the military, and reminded us that the air, even more than the water, can be unforgiving of the slightest mistake. I wondered, then, how that was possible.

But when I leapt off the platform during my first jump, I was pulled out of the door into a wall of air that tossed me from side to side like a wave at the beach. It pushed against me on all sides: there was no up, no down, I was just falling, free, waiting, waiting.

I counted to four: the amount of time it should take for the parachute to deploy. One thousand, two thousand, three thou—and I was pulled sharply upwards. I looked up to check my canopy, making sure that the parachute had opened correctly and had not folded in on itself or wrapped up like a long, thin stick. I gained canopy control and floated slowly towards the ground, slower than the men who had jumped out behind me. Parachutes make lighter people fall softer, following—yet also, it seemed to me—defying the laws of gravity, physics.

I pulled my parachute lines deep into my chest, away from the wind, in order to slow my descent. I landed, hard. The force of it pushed my helmet forward, scraping and bruising my nose. Sand sprayed into my eyes, mouth, and ears. But before I could breathe, my parachute caught a gust of wind and dragged me on my back across the drop zone. Finally, I was able to release myself from the harness.

I considered the jumpmaster's warning. The air, more than the sea, can be unforgiving of the slightest mistake. Now I begged to differ. It was the land itself that didn't forgive. Leaping out of the aircraft and into the air, I had been buffeted by gusts of wind. When my parachute deployed I was yanked upwards, a small discomfort. And as I floated to the ground, I drifted slowly from side to side. But upon landing, I hit the ground and the ground did not give. I bounced, hard. The ground did not mold around my body on impact, but remained firm, solid.

Perhaps I am, like many other Americans, too accustomed to the idea of earth as giver; giver of life, food, water. That the earth as a whole gives and forgives. We know a forest fire started by a cigarette butt may burn hundreds of acres; however we rely on the earth to rebuild herself, giving back to us what we lost.

But is it really nature's place to be forthcoming, to replace herself as we dry up her resources, overdraw her ground water, overlog her forests, and dump chemicals into her air? The Earth refreshes, renews, and replaces minerals, fish, water, and air with more minerals, fish, water, and air. The cycle seems endless, but what happens when the fresh water has dried up? Where do we turn? What do we do when the earth stops giving?

We can try to break our fall; grab the parachute lines and struggle against our atmosphere of consumption. We would survive, despite a few breaks and bruises. Or we can continue on our accelerating course, directly into the unforgiving ground.

I stood up, brushing dust and sand off my uniform, my neck, out of my hair. I had survived this jump, and knew I would jump again. I gathered my parachute, slung it onto my back, and began to walk toward the collection point. From here, my destination looked so far away.

DEBORAH FRIES

Hartsfield-Atlanta Baggage Claim

At first I think they're clapping for an employee of the month
I tell the man beside me at dinner, explaining what happened
earlier that day, how airport employees led the formation
through baggage claim, how everyone turned, many clapped,
but I'd been confused, my gaze stuck on a young blonde with
glasses who must have been the age I was when I was traveling
between bases, although I wore nylons and Air Force pumps,
and looked in my seersucker more like a flight attendant for
a cheap airline than someone quota-picked to triage the
dismembered in rice paddies. This woman, I tell him, and all
her squad were fat with gear, weighted down with the new
camouflage clearly not meant for duck hunting or jungles—
the mossy greens, rotting swamp colors we wore replaced
with lighter, fractal desert patterns, everything the shades
of sand. He sips wine, touches my arm. *I go up to them,* he
says, *tell them I wish them well, but they should get out now,
and I'll help them.* He talks about Lynndie England, Graner
and Sivits, about people with what he calls *limitations.* I say
Sivits grew up in Hyndman, just 20 miles away. But I don't tell
him—here in our conference of poets and writers, dining
in a fake Polynesian hut, wearing denim and trying to dodge
enemies of anonymity and arterial plaque—all I know of
limitations and how it feels to be stuck in the Alleghenies,
unemployed, returned in winter with your parents pissed,
refusing to pay for even community college after your last
fiasco, nothing left at nineteen but ignominy and the crazy
catapult of your own body into something wild and stupid,
like a mosh pit or monsoon. *What did you do? Did you clap?*

Can't he see how I grew up avoiding people like that crew
from Abu Ghraib in my high school cafeteria, watched them
climb onto buses at the end of the day while I walked home—
a college-bound townie, with her art supplies and no plans
to go to war? Sense how easily I could be seduced to stay or
enlist, needing—more than the adventure of Southeast Asia—
parents who would barricade me with their bodies, arm me
with love? Can he picture, here in this dark hotel restaurant,
how one spring day, lacking everything I needed, I slipped out
of one world and entered another, forgotten, to rise at five
in the pink, Texas pre-dawn, march in formation past the WAF
commander's house, saluting and singing her favorite song,
Tiny Bubbles, morning after morning, without applause?

SHARON D. ALLEN

New Definition of Dirt

Every mission we've been on has been worse than the one before. In terms of living conditions, anyway. Because we're horizontal engineers, sometimes we build the camps. So there's absolutely nothing there when we arrive: no port-a-johns, no showers. You know you're not exactly at the Hyatt when an outhouse with a burn barrel would be an improvement. A vast improvement.

I thought we got dirty at my first camp. I didn't know the definition of "dirty" until we went to our next. This was another whole league of dirty. We stayed in a nearly demolished house previously owned by Uday Hussein himself. It was missing its rear wall. When the dozers were working, or when the wind was blowing, the dirt was like fog. One day I even thought I saw clouds in the sky. Nope. It was dirt.

I woke up every morning covered with dirt, with dirt boogers and dirt drymouth. The first few days we were content with bottle showers, but we needed a full-on naked shower by day four. My buddy Kim Predmore and I parked a D9 uparmored dozer perpendicular to another one, hung the shower bags on the doors and dragged pallets over to stand on. Probably the best shower I ever had.

I maintain that at jobsites like this one, there's no reason to take our weapons on the dozers with us. In about fifteen minutes they're too dirty to function, anyway. Day two, Wiley said, "I would so shoot myself in the face right now, if my weapon would fire, which it won't." I thought of making a great escape on a D7 dozer. I'd just jump on and keep driving until I hit Kuwait.

We knew we were going to be here for a while. And we knew that we might have another camp to build after this one. I could just picture it: they would come to get us in three years and we'd have turned into mountain men. Maybe someone like Morgan would have wandered off.

We'd spot him roaming the countryside, herding sheep and muttering to himself. All the guys would have full neckbeards, wearing swaddling clothes, crusty with dirt, and barefoot. We would have our own esoteric accent, perhaps our own language. We'd be living off the land, trapping camel spiders and lizards for food, worshipping our own god, a combination of Nordic dirt god and Akhenaton's sun god, Aton. We'd offer him sacrificial water bottles.

III.

WEAPONS TIGHT

An order to err on the side of caution; to fire only at targets recognized as hostile.

VICTORIA A. HUDSON, LTC

Convoy Day

What I remember most about convoy day is the sweat. Not the *perspiration,* not the *glow,* and not the *glistening sheen.* I am drenched in salty fluid that rolls off my face and down the small of my back in a river of diminishing hydration.

Under my ballistic armor vest, my gloves, and my helmet, my long-sleeved uniform shirt is drenched clear through. I have soaked the T-shirt layer and the outer shirt layer, even every inch of sleeve. I wear a head scarf to absorb the sweat that rolls from under the helmet, stinging and obscuring my vision. I have a little teeny head and use a kid's pirate kerchief I found in Key West. I never knew I could sweat so much. I keep waiting for someone to tell me I can't wear the little black and white kerchief, but so far, no one screws with me about it. The few of us who go outside the wire on a regular basis have earned a little juice to push the boundaries.

Preparation begins the night before convoy day, when I lay out all my gear. There is the 26-pound ballistic vest (bought for me by my friends back home as a hedge against the Army failing to provide one), which has 90 rounds of M4 carbine ammunition and 90 rounds of 9mm ammunition attached. There is a three-pound First Aid kit containing all kinds of things I barely know how to use. I've got high-tech bandages made from shellfish that induce clotting, brand new tourniquets that require only one hand to use (useful if the other is blown off), as well as loads of other nifty items. I've had a 40-hour class compressed into two and a half days, which is supposed to certify me as a Combat Life Saver (more commonly referred to by the guys on the line as Combat Life Taker). None of the tools in my high-tech First Aid kit were mentioned in that class.

And in true Murphy's Law fashion, my plan for preparation fails. I forget my ballistic sunglasses. I go back to the hooches to retrieve them.

Two minutes before the departure briefing I figure out what else I forgot: my extra ammunition. Ninety rounds won't last long in a firefight; maybe a minute. I have a bag with an additional six magazines, each with 30 rounds. Fortunately, I'm able to grab from the security office an extra seven mags already filled with ammo. But running late screws with my frame of mind. I've missed breakfast, too.

The whole team comes together at convoy brief. We gather around the vehicle and the Convoy Sergeant reviews the route and what to do if a vehicle gets hit by an improvised explosive device (IED). Using rocks, we go over what happens. Each rock is a vehicle. If Victor One gets hit, each vehicle will do X, Y or Z. Victor Two, for example, secures the damaged vehicle for recovery. Victor Three engages the enemy as needed. And if Victor 2 gets hit, each vehicle will do Y, Z or X. We work our way through each vehicle. Eventually, we upgrade these demonstrations and use toy Bigfoot trucks instead of rocks. Even so, we continue calling this the Rock Drill.

I am in charge of the last vehicle in the line. Our job is to secure the rear of the convoy. That means our gunner stands in the turret, facing the road behind us. There are two types of people on the convoy: those of us that do this often and those who are just along for the ride. For them, the convoy is only a tool. For them, we are a very well armed chauffeur service. These passengers like to think they know what they are doing when they leave the safe-walled compound. They don't need to comply with our rules for doing things. They ask why when there is no time to explain. They put their bags on top of the ammo cans that are laid out for the gunner between the rear seats, and then wonder aloud why the gunner gets pissed and kicks everything off when he discovers this. One would think that when you go outside the wire where people may shoot at you or try to blow you up with a suicide vehicle, keeping the ammo clear for easy access would be a no-brainer.

Once we are in the vehicles we radio check with all the other vehicles, receive authorization and move out. When we reach the edge of the camp, we lock and load our weapons. We turn on electronic devices that emit a jamming signal to countermeasure the IEDs that are designed to be detonated by someone hiding nearby as we drive past. We can't do much about the ones that explode when you roll over them. And off we go.

Iraqi citizens are required to stop their vehicles or pull to the far side of the road when they see us coming. If they get too close, the gunners will shoot at the road in front of them. We use hand signals and yell at the drivers to back off. If we have to shoot, the gunner will pop a round or two at the car engine, in front of the driver. If the gunner is convinced of an imminent threat of a suicide driver, the guy is going to get lit up: bad guy burnt toast. Inside our vehicle we are enclosed in a couple of tons of armor. Windows up, we are encased in a mobile sauna. The air-conditioning works like a charm; a strong blast of hot air, recycled from outside, which adds about 30 degrees to our already sweltering cavern of a vehicle.

If attacked, we do not shoot. Only the exposed gunner in the turret fires back. We will not open the windows or doors for anything other than to rescue buddies in a blown up or disabled vehicle. Even the tiniest crack for fresh air would leave a place for fragments to penetrate. The driver drives, the gunner guns, the rest in the vehicle are lookouts. The gunners are the ones really on the line. They do the shooting but they can get their heads ripped off by invisible wires strung across the road, or have an incendiary grenade lit on their heads when going under a bridge. When we get to these overpasses, we zigzag, never exiting aligned with where we entered. We tell the gunner to duck. As in war movies when an officer will "call the ball" to announce a plane coming in to land on the carrier, I have taken to "calling the duck" for our gunner.

We look for unusual trash, strange wires hanging off an overpass, cars that do not seem to be moving fast enough, or those that look too heavy in the rear. Along the way we keep up a running commentary.

"Vehicle on the right. Bus at 3 o'clock. Obstacle in the road. Right turn. Traffic circle left. Truck moving on the left. Overpass in 5 . . . 4 . . . 3 . . . 2 . . . duck!"

We drive fast and furious down the middle of the road, weaving from side to side, avoiding, staying clear of obstacles or vehicles that have pulled over. Part of this ongoing monologue is to provide what we call situational awareness to everyone in the vehicle. Each person has a designated sector to watch, and isn't supposed to be looking elsewhere.

As we get deeper into the downtown district, the blocks seem to be arranged like a grocery store. First a block of butcher shops with carcasses hanging from hooks, then a block with fruit stalls and carts.

Next is a textile block with bolts of cloth and clothes, then the hardware section with little shops with tools, parts, and plumbing fixtures. People are crowded everywhere. An old woman in traditional garb carries a plastic bag with groceries in one hand and a stuffed purple dinosaur in the other.

We arrive at the Provincial Government Building, pulling into gates between 12-foot walls strung with concertina wire. The Iraqi police guard the entrance, and there is a machine gun nest atop the building we are visiting. Next door are two 12-story structures.

We had a plan for dismounting the passengers. I was to lead the internal security team and act as the Commander's bodyguard. But the Commander, Lone Ranger that he is, has ditched his security team. By the time my vehicle pulls into the parking lot, everyone from the other trucks has already entered the building.

The security team sets up to wait outside. We have a gunner on top of each vehicle, and the rest of us are dismounted at various positions around the parking lot. A two-soldier team is doing a security site assessment, so two more are with them as guards while the others walk around and take pictures. I am watching the many sniper possibilities above us while patrolling with the team doing the security assessment. We look for snipers all the time when outside our compound, which is significantly more nerve-wracking when we're not armored up in a vehicle impenetrable to gunfire.

Providing security means patrolling and watching everywhere: up, down, and all around. We are in a city; outside the government compound walls there are shops and street stalls. Some areas remind me of Telegraph Avenue in Berkeley near the University of California, or a flea market with vendors lined along the street. More importantly, there is lots of open space, packed tight with people.

After a few hours in 117-degree heat, my uniform has become an oversaturated sponge and I am a puddle of exhaustion, weighed down with 75 pounds of armor, gear, and ammo. I stand by a low, white masonry wall, angling for the tiniest bit of shade from a scraggly bush with a single odd white flower. My eyes are clouding over. I can't think, I feel my body swaying, I no longer see anything in my sector except what is right in front of me. I back up against the wall, seeking its solidity. The untrimmed branches of the bush surround me. I take a pull through the hydration tube on my shoulder and swallow tepid water. Taking a step away from the wall, I sway forward and almost go down.

Fuck, I think. *Fuck, fuck, fuck.* I am the senior ranking person out here on this security detail and about to fall over on this, my very first out-the-wire mission, with apparent heat exhaustion. What kind of shit ass, goat rope, fucked-up situation is that?

I spend a few more minutes trying to tough it out. I start to argue with myself.

Going to the medic is going to suck.

Falling on my face is going to suck even more.

Go to the medic.

No, tough it out. Cowboy up, Major.

I sway so far forward I have to catch myself with a giant stride of my boot. I sink back into the wall.

Which is more humiliating, falling down in full combat gear without a shot fired, or going to the medic and saying you think the heat is getting to you?

I lose the tough-guy argument with myself.

I walk over to the medic. "I'm feeling the heat."

Two soldiers on break in the shade look my way. Slowly, they look away. Slowly, they gather up their gear and move back to their vehicles.

The medic looks at me. "Sit down in the shade," she says, pointing.

I sit. "How much water have you had?" she asks. She takes my pulse. I tell her I've had 5 liters already and pissed out semi clear. She looks at me some more. "What did you have for breakfast?"

What breakfast? I missed breakfast. Now she looks at me like I'm an idiot. "Got an MRE?"

I pull one out of my cargo pocket. Thirty minutes later I've consumed a cold concoction of meat and sauce, some ranger pudding (cocoa powder mixed with water, sugar, and coffee creamer) and crackers with cheese spread. Hooah, I'm ready to go. I feel like someone should order me to my room after duty to write a thousand times *I will not skip breakfast on convoy day ever again.*

I've been back on my post a couple of hours. We've rotated everyone through eating and resting in the shade. The heat is relentless. Even with the ballistic glasses, the glare bouncing off the concrete is searing our eyes.

"Where the hell are they?" one of the Sergeants says. The meeting was supposed to last no more than an hour. "What is taking so damn friggin' long?"

"They were due out five hours ago," the Top-Sergeant grumbles, adding a few choice expletives.

All the pictures have been shot and the team sector has sketched all the possible sniper posts, dead zones, and locals' guard posts. The ice is long past melted in the coolers packed into the rear of each truck. The image of the "this is your brain on drugs" frying pan sits in my head. We are getting slack and tired.

Suddenly, the local guards, Iraqi police in thin cotton shirts of light blue that remind me of American bus drivers, mount up their little white pickup trucks. There are three men in the front of each, and a gunner in the rear with a half dozen or more guys perched around him. They're riding civilian Toyota or Isuzu pickups, like those tooling down any highway at home. The whole thing looks crazy: a big .50 caliber machine gun mounted on a pole that's been soldered in the middle of the bed. Men hang on like keystone cops. The trucks peel out of the parking lot.

"Soooooo, this doesn't look good," says one of our soldiers. We've been hearing intermittent shots all morning, but shots are an everyday experience. We gather closer to our trucks, nervously scanning. A long half hour passes.

"What the fuck!" one of our gunners calls out. The passengers have finally come out from the building. Only they aren't coming back to the vehicles.

Our passengers and some of the Iraqis, a group of 20 or so men, are tromping out the gate and across the road with only a few Iraqi policemen providing their security.

"Where are they going?" someone asks. Without bothering to inform the external security team, our guys are taking a little walk to the annex building, outside the gate and across the busy, double-lane intersection. My heart is pumping hard.

"Mount up!" Top yells.

We scramble into our Hummers. "Victor Two, cover the intersection! Victor Three and Four, take the lead and set up across the street. Victor One will take the corner and Victor Five the gate." We peel out to our new sectors.

The street outside the wall is teeming with people, as busy as a packed farmer's market. Storefronts and vendor stalls are everywhere. People surround us; looming above are two- and three-story buildings containing offices and residences. We take over the street, forcing the locals onto the sidewalk, but we cannot control the high ground. Children try to approach us; a few brave vendors attempt to offer us food and goods. We motion them back with abrupt English and menacing gestures with our weapons. We were given little laminated cheat sheets with Arabic phrases for this purpose. No one remembers how to pronounce the words.

Scents fill the air. Roasting chicken, broiled meat hung on hooks, and fresh bread. I'm still hungry. Colors are brilliant. Shades of grey, tan, brown, brick, splashes of color from textiles, fruit piled on tables, toys. Every object is more defined, every color sharper. I hear individual voices from a dozen Arabic conversations. The smallest movement attracts my attention.

I wonder why I don't have any sense of fear in this, my first honest-to-God potential combat situation. I'm surrounded by people, any one of whom could set off an ambush on the Americans out here in the open. Am I numb, or am I in a state of invigoration? Any second could bring the crack of rifle fire, the ping of rounds ricocheting, the whistle of incoming fire. I wonder why I want someone to shoot.

RACHEL VIGIL

Stay in Your Lane

Four American soldiers at the gate
stricken, confused, 9/11 fingers on safeties
tiny fists to a breast

The runner charges into the female Army tent at one a.m.
terrorist, North Gate, 18-wheeler
need Arabic linguist
I assemble myself in darkness, basic training speed
running to the waiting HMMWV
A whiff of diesel, Arabic words for
semi, purpose, gate and forbidden line up
with sand in my mouth
باب الخارجي ,شاهنة أللوري , سبب , ممنوع

The Egyptian delivery man
stands near his truck
explaining to well-fed soldiers
a poor-man's situation
His truck is full of lettuce from Cairo
just as he says
the regular shipment to feed our soldiers—

Hoping to calm the guards
I say
he is only sleeping in his truck
between five hour drives
being paid too little
for delivering our food on schedule

I turn to him
أفوان يا أخي
we are not human enough
to let you rest between journeys outside our gate
You're safer
sprawled in your seat
a klick down the road

ELAINE LITTLE TUMAN

Edit and Spin

Noor Alim, the detainee, lay on an operating table at the Ghazni Fire Base with burn wounds to his chest, one eye gravely injured and leaking a clear fluid, and battered hands that resembled little claws. The commander had asked that I interrogate him before the sedatives rendered him incapable of talking.

I assembled my interrogation paperwork and obtained clearance from the doctor to speak to Noor. He was surprisingly lucid when I began the questioning.

His story was that he was a teacher who had been coerced by a local Taliban leader named Ali Mohammad to place an improvised explosive device (IED) on the road. Noor feared for his family's safety if he didn't comply. But as the story continued I found a lot of holes. First, the name Ali Mohammad is about as common as John Smith. Second, Noor had been picked up after being injured by the IED in an extremely remote area. It was not a place where there was much traffic of either the Afghan or American military variety. Noor maintained that Ali Mohammad had told him not to place the IED in a specific area, but just to place it anywhere in order to send a message that the Taliban was present. But he couldn't explain how the message was supposed to have gotten out even if the explosion had gone off as planned. "Was there going to be an announcement?" I asked. He had no answer. Noor also claimed that he had actually been trying to rid himself of the IED and had injured himself during a disposal attempt. The entire story had a piecemeal quality to it that made it difficult to know whether Noor or the sedatives were talking.

It is the interrogator's duty to go through all the information given by the detainee and then go back and plug in any holes in the narrative. In other words, you were to follow any question to the bitter end. You kept asking and then what? And then where? And then why? And then how? And then who? You did this until the detainee had nothing further he could say.

I did the best I could, shooting off questions rapidly with the excellent support of the Ghazni interpreter, Sam, who jumped in with suggestions for rephrasing for clarity and conciseness. Sam spoke Pashto and Dari, the two main languages of Afghanistan. We worked well as a team. The second I finished a question, he translated. The moment Noor Alim answered, Sam interpreted, and I wrote down the words quickly.

That night, Sam invited me to a dinner party in his quarters. He supplemented the meager dining hall fare with a barbecue featuring kabobs and fresh vegetables. The food was delicious but Sam was too busy to talk. He was busy chaperoning Jamila, his niece, who had invited a date to the party. He sat beside the couple as they watched a Bollywood movie on DVD.

Jamila was exquisite-looking young woman with a face like a Persian miniature. She was resisting an arranged marriage in America set up by her parents. Their extended family had been part of a large Afghan-American community in Omaha, Nebraska.

"She fled Nebraska and came home to Kabul," Sam told me. He had somehow been granted permission to pick her up in Kabul and bring her back to the base, where she was living under an unusual arrangement made possible by a combination of relaxed rules at this small fire base and, I suspected, sympathy over her plight. Sam and his niece were close: he had introduced her to the young man with whom she'd fallen in love. "They want to get married," Sam said. "We are trying to get permission from Jamila's parents, back in Omaha."

Later I met Jamila in the hallway. She showed me her room, unpacking a series of glitzy caftans she had bought in Ghazni.

When it finally became apparent that a drugged sleep was the only thing that Noor Alim was capable of pulling off, we left him alone. I was oddly exhilarated as I walked to the tent to compose my report. I had never had the chance to interrogate someone so soon after a crime had been committed. I was able to get fresh information without the filter of time or contemplation. I typed up the report and waited for my flight, hoping that my recommendation for Alim to be transported back to Bagram for further questioning would be followed. The recommendation made sense, because he had already implicated himself. The transfer to Bagram would be to his benefit because the quality of the medical care at that base would greatly surpass that which he would get from local doctors.

But if Noor Alim was sent back he would need an escort. I asked the flight line supervisors if I could do the job. I told them that since Noor's medic flight would leave the base later than the flight I was originally scheduled to take, I would have more time to polish my report. That's what I said, but the truth was I wanted to be there with him. I received permission and prepared for the flight to Bagram.

Before I left, I was asked by a group of soldiers if I wanted to see a "demolition derby." Their mission was to blow up captured caches of ammunition. I said yes, mainly because I knew Sam was their interpreter. Our earlier conversation about his niece had intrigued me.

The ammunition, which had been recovered from people's houses or turned in or confiscated by US forces, was lined up in little rows. Members of the Afghan National Army were doing the majority of the heavy lifting while the American soldiers supervised. As we watched, Sam filled me in about his life in Nebraska and his job and family. He was an attractive man with a compact build and warm brown eyes. He nodded and glanced at me as he spoke, and asked thoughtful questions. His English was excellent and his accent faint; he had immigrated to the United States in 1980, shortly after the Soviet invasion of Afghanistan. He worked as an engineer back in Nebraska, which sounded important and well paying, but I figured this interpreter gig was probably even more lucrative. He mentioned a wife and two young daughters back home, but when I asked more questions he finessed the conversation away from them.

Once the ammunition was all laid out we repaired to a safe place to watch everything ignite. The explosions lit up the landscape with a series of miniature mushroom clouds.

Dawn was approaching. The medical helicopter landed and Noor Alim was lifted on a gurney onto the aircraft. I glanced back at the main building and saw a shadowy figure lurking nearby. It was Sam, who saw me but said nothing. I climbed up and settled in for the ride. The medic made some weak jokes about the state of the patient. Nothing to joke about, really, but I understood. I liked to watch the way the medics work on the injured. There was a gentleness to it. I took a photograph.

I saw Noor Alim again less than two months later. He sat in front of an interpreter and me for his first post-hospital interrogation, his debilitating injuries now a permanent part of him.

"Do you recognize me?" I asked. "I interviewed you after the IED blew up in your face. It is very important that you tell us exactly what happened, and we will try to help you." But my concern barely registered.

His medical care had been good by Afghan standards. Although his appearance was scary, his wounds were in check. He made a sudden move towards the interpreter and me and we both pushed our chairs back. It was not an aggressive move—he was only readjusting his position—but we were taken off guard. Then Noor insisted on sitting on the floor because, he said, it hurt less. His story had changed dramatically, as I knew it would. In the interim there had been time to edit and spin.

The day I watched the ammunition demolition derby, a group of Kuchis, a nomadic tribe of Afghanistan, descended on the scene from out of nowhere as soon as the explosions stopped. They ignored the American soldiers yelling at them: some of the ammunition could still explode. They raced to pick up the precious scrap metal, their colorful robes flapping in the wind.

RACHEL VIGIL

Deployment

18 September 2001:
work in civilian clothes, gas mask in briefcase
our Cairo hotel a majestic palace
marble floors, lush grounds
soft rooms converted into offices
banquet tables-cum-desks

Collect, translate, deadline
a steady flow of coffee
makes this space the innards
of any DC building.
The shock of the tower bombings
reels us in tight

Pyramids forgotten, I take in the rest
through the focused eyes of the mission.
Translate,
my third eye locates the other desert-clad soldiers
sweating and nervous in flak jackets,
in tents miles around me, knowing nothing but
guesses, rumors
while tourists here wear flip-flops and ride camels

We dine under glinting crystal
white embroidered linens, the slow arrival
of a garlic and lemoned meal
in courses,
reminding me to refocus
savor the day and its reprieve
the weightless gown.

Choose words carefully over elegant china
sanitize shop talk
all three hang our speech mid-sentence
at the approach of waiters, dressing in a silence that we—
arms, legs, hands of a larger organism
have ceased to feel awkward about
as we practice
holding back.

Watch a local couple eating,
their lives moving in real time
luxuriously out of reach
her voice a gentle lace,
she practices saying a word or phrase
less than he is hoping for
all of him leans to all of her

She wears pale pink
a color I always detested
watered-down and weak, but like men here
I have come to appreciate it
delicate
in a land of hard soil, earthen buildings
a sun that melts everything
to its simplest elements.

IV.

COMING IN HOT

Dangerous and intense, as under enemy fire. To arrive with guns blazing.

Stretcher I

Lying on his back, both lungs collapsed,
a storekeeper loses his goods.
Legs crushed, hip crushed, barely a breath
left in his massive chest,
he cannot call out for help.
Help believes it has already come,
has already delivered him from below
the crumbled decks of a smoldering ship,
has gone to carry on the wild salvage.
He can only look into the dark
depths of the eyes that greet him,
eyes as dark as his own, skin almost as brown
as his own Trini cocoa. He can only smell
burning fuel, burning flesh,
consider the threatening mass
of a scimitar
on his thick, weak-pulsed neck;
he knows his size
cannot protect him
from its silvered edge, and in the man
who wields it he sees
the men and women who can no longer
wield a thing. Goods lost:
1 wedding ring.   1 class ring.   1 gold necklace.
1 gold watch.   2 diamond studs.

KHADIJAH QUEEN

Stretcher II

An engineman
who will not make it.
Who catches the eye
of the storekeeper next to him
when he takes his last breath.
When he takes his last breath,
a young man laughs:
"You are dead, American!" he shouts
into a bleeding ear, snatches
ring and watch and golden
cross, runs into smoke
and crowd and flight.

TERRY HURLEY

The Dead Iraqi Album

My ten-year old son never asks about what I write. He came home from school last week, told me about his day, then quietly went over to the sunroom couch and sat with his book, stretching out his legs, propping his feet on the arm. Our family cat joined him. The only sound in the room was the turning of pages, mine and his.

His pages were homework. Mine were the Dead Iraqi Album, as we used to call it back in Kuwait. It sold on the streets for $5.00. One of my enlisted soldiers picked it up for me: a gift of sorts. When I first received the album, I wasn't shocked. I was caught up in it. It was exhilarating to see bodies burnt and blown apart. These people were trying to kill us, after all.

In the first few pages the images are tame: burned tanks, oil fires blazing in the background, smoke billowing overhead. There are pages and pages of oil fires. As I looked at the photos, I could almost feel it on my skin, like baby oil, but pungent. I'd led a Troposcatter Radio team at the airport in Kuwait, when the smoke from oil fires covered the sky, turning day into night. The album opens with images of burned vehicles. There is an enemy prisoner of war encampment encircled with concertina wire. And Iraqi soldiers standing in lines or sitting apart from each other, no doubt waiting for transport to a permanent camp where they can receive food, shelter, and a place to pray.

Earlier today, I took these photos out of the closet to write about how they made me feel. I guess we all wanted to see the carnage. We wanted to participate on a more personal level in the defeat of the enemy force. Too long in the desert, we wanted proof we were really there for the liberation of Kuwait's people and not for another paperwork-ridden training exercise. Unlike the front line forces, we were too far away to feel the heat, the anticipation of battle. Our mission was support. I guess the photos brought us closer, helped us understand. It was a different time. War makes us different people. I sat in my living room, fixed on images of the dead, focused on my past life, on my days as a Lieutenant in the Arabian Desert.

Suddenly my son was looking at a photo over my shoulder. Quickly, I closed the album. I hadn't been paying attention to where he was.

He seemed frightened by my reaction. "Boo, its okay," I said. "Mom is looking at some pictures that you shouldn't see just yet. Someday, when you are a little older, I will tell you all about them."

How condescending this must have sounded to my gifted boy. He started to walk away.

"Listen," I said. "The pictures I'm looking at are very graphic. They're gross, but in a bad way. They are pictures of real people, real dead people." He had never seen a corpse. When his grandfather died, we chose not to take him to the viewing. His brown eyes looked confused. How could I tell him that still, after all these years, I had bad dreams, that I was still haunted?

"The pictures in this album were taken during a war," I said. "Real war is not like one of your video games. It's a dark, brutal, experience. Some of the men in here have died in horrible ways. Like burning to death or being run over like animals."

He was silent. "Can I play with my friends now?" he finally said.

As a child, I took little interest in my father's war stories. Why should he be any different? "Sure, Honey . . . home by six." I smiled. "Don't forget your cell phone."

In the album are nine photos of dead enemy soldiers. Some have been burned alive in their vehicles. Several are still grasping their weapons, as if clinging to hope that they might still defeat coalition forces. They look like special effects, like a television crime scene before the police arrive with their yellow tape. The bodies are in contorted positions, if they are whole. Most are not. They reminded me of some large fallen animal I might see on a busy highway, one a semi truck has met with and passed over on a dark night. These bodies were not people; they were the enemy. They were Iraqi soldiers working for a man that was no less than a monster. We had become numb to the images of death. We felt nothing. Some soldiers had posters of Saddam they would throw darts at. It was us versus them.

In the world where I grew up, this brutality was unimaginable. Yet there I was, enjoying photos of death, death of human beings. What had I become? What had that country done to me?

My stepson is seventeen. He is the image of his father, the retired Colonel, minus a few gray hairs and some well-earned Army muscle. This past summer, he spoke of attending a military college. For the education, he told me, and for the opportunity to serve his country. At his request, I sent away for a West Point information packet. I tell myself he will be trained well, that he will become a warrior, that he will face adversity with strength and courage. I tell myself that he will grow mentally and physically. He will become a better person, an officer who is passionate and dedicated like his father . . . maybe even nurturing and supportive like his stepmother. Like our fathers did for us, we will give him the chance to excel at something greater than the individual.

I will never show my stepson the album of the dead. If you focus on the death and carnage of battle, it is all you see. I believe he should concentrate on mission completion, on his capabilities and those of his soldiers. He should put all his effort into the positive end result.

No, the album must remain hidden, a memory of a time before baseball practice and family camping trips, when my maternal urges were satisfied by personally delivering to my soldiers their letters from home.

I have kept the album for so many years now. I cannot bring myself to destroy it. Besides being a symbol of my survival, it is also a reminder of what human beings are capable of. In some strange way, it makes me more grateful to be where I am now, to live in a country where I don't have to sleep with my rifle or worry about imminent chemical and biological attacks. I hope the album is found long after my husband and I are gone, in a time when there is such peace in this world that its contents are tossed aside as unimaginable, its blurred images lost in obscurity, because in this future time there are no weapons of war, of destruction. There is no need for warriors.

My stepdaughter is twenty-two and heading to Africa with the Peace Corps. Her mission, as she tells me, is to empower young women, teach them to take care of themselves, become independent. I mentioned the album to her, and asked if she wanted to see. "Yuck," she said. "No!"

At her age, I had already served four years. I had already experienced so much. I know we've sheltered her. She has never seen hardship. She has never been to a country where swarms of children beg for food. I wish I could be there to help her through this journey, to guide her through the dark times. When she returns, two years from now, she will be so different. She will no longer be the protected, wide-eyed, little girl I remember. She may have memories that torment her. She will survive . . . and she will return a stronger woman.

Until today, my photos of the Iraqi dead were packed in an old suitcase next to an oil-stained Kuwaiti flag and some Desert Storm trading cards, mementos of a time when good defended against evil. For years, my experience there cloaked me in some strange shawl. Numb to the sting of war, I felt an emptiness, as if I'd cried too much and had no more tears to shed. Yet actually I had not cried at all. I became the quiet one in the room. I struggled daily to focus on life away from the intensity of war, on a peaceful existence, on family. From the security of my home, I watched and I listened. I ached to be a part of the fight again, to hold my rifle, to feel the sting of the desert sand upon my skin, the anticipation, the urgency of facing the enemy. I had become so much more than I once was, so aware.

My son stood at the door to my bedroom. "Can I sleep with you?" His father was away on work trip. He looked as if he needed cuddle time.

He put his head on the pillow. "Why do you have a photo album of dead people?"

"You know mom went to war." I thought he had forgotten about it. "Why do you think I kept the album?"

"I don't know . . . to remind you how bad war is?"

"Well," I said, "what do you think I should do with it now?"

He was silent for a moment. "I don't think you need it anymore. You got out of the Army. Why do you need to remember the bad things? Don't just throw it out though. Someone may find it. Maybe you should donate it to some war museum."

I held him. "What a great idea. I promise I'll see if anyone wants it."

None of the bodies in the Dead Iraqi Album has a recognizable face, save one. He wears no uniform. He lays face up, as if he has been in some horrible street fight. He needs a shave. His clothes are filthy, but otherwise, I see no sign that he is even dead. There is a Pepsi can with Arabic lettering on the dirt next to the body. Of them all, this one is the only one that someone might have recognized. Someone might have seen his face, and mourned his loss.

I remember my soldiers. I remember meeting the man who would become my husband. I remember the cheering crowds as I led my troops into Kuwait.

VICTORIA A. HUDSON, LTC

Bosnia 1996

How
In mere words
Selectively chosen
Do I fill a void
Created with
Harmless, honest, polite, true
Inquiry?

What was it like?

Imagine
Your home
Your mother's home
Your mother's mother's home
Your home
Vast holes torn throughout
Mortar and wood
Bricks crumbling
Every shard of glass
Carpets the ground
Submerging every blade
of grass

All around
Every building
Every neighbor
And neighbor's neighbor
Firebombed
Roofs caving in

As far as you can see
Silver dollar holes pockmark
Whitewashed walls
Crunch
Of pulverized glass
The only sound
Compressed with every step

This avoidable horror
of destruction
No excusable
Act of God
Hurricane
Earthquake
Tornado
Only the intolerance
One human for another
What was it like?

My voice lost in
The vice grip of tumultuous emotion
Eyes welling
As in front of me
A family ripped apart
One hundred meters and more
Cold water flows laced with mines
Iron girders twisted, torn
Breached
The gaping mouth of nothing where
Once cement and stone brought passage

Speck of people, ant-bodies
Shouting
Waving
Jumping
Barely seen, unheard
This parody of communication

Their only link
Across this river
Border, boundary, barrier
For this mother, father, brother, son, daughter, sister,
lover

How do I convey
My obscene witness to their pain?
And you ask
What was it like?

JUDITH K. BOYD

The Joust

In my dream
an Iraqi woman approaches my Humvee
silent tears
sick baby in outstretched arms
I reach to take the child
it begins to wail—

fumble with gas mask
pull it over head
fingers thick and clumsy with fog of sleep

the siren wails
heart pounds, I'm cowering on bed
no time to run for the bunker

a Scud rushes to me
explosives dipped in chemicals
I will dissolve

the surge of the Patriot
a white knight released
my future is sport

missile and rocket
each in pursuit
racing toward the other

a distant explosion is over the desert
I remove my mask and bow

KHADIJAH QUEEN

35 x 36

for GSM1

who fell out of that gash
    burning

who pushed and was pushed,
                  shock-shook, skin

falling from her face   like debris

whose adrenaline
     slowed the salt-sting
of seawater bathing her

     muscles, unraveling
in tiny ribbons—

who felt screams
welling in her throat, the sound of tons
of steel   bending
as the world   went silent

who saved a man twice her size
and only in so doing
saved
herself—

BOBBI DYKEMA KATSANIS

Desert Storm

across the wintry, desiccated dark
a telephone bleats,
reveals not voice
but lightning strike of pain,
shrieking howls of agony
like they'd sacrificed her son.

she did not need an ambulance,
firefighters, or police—
but a world that could make sense,
where children were not sent
eight thousand miles
with guns to aim at children,
where days to honor men of peace
were not defiled by mortar rounds
exploding into flesh,
where rippling desert
vultures did not dance
over fresh human carrion.

where giant deadly jellyfish
had not unfurled across Hiroshima sky
or billowed in the wind.
the sirens' keening
for another desert mother's son.

"it is finished,"
is what we thought he said.
which was ridiculous,
for it had just begun.

V.

ENEMY IN THE RANKS

A person who puts the group at risk in order to gain personal or tactical advantage.

CHRISTY L. CLOTHIER

The Controller

After my shift in the air traffic control tower, a white van pockmarked with red rust dropped me and the other females at our row of particle-board trailers. Here at Naval Air Station San Clemente Island, the women lived in transitional housing; most of the men slept in permanent bar-racks with the senior enlisted. The van departed down a steep dirt road to the base center near the docks, cutting us off from the rest of the island.

Separation from everything else shrunk us into a tight female com-munity that found entertainment wherever we could. Without television or radio, and sharing a single outdoor phone, our after-hours activi-ties usually involved alcohol. That night most of the female controllers planned to test the theory of beer being good for our hair.

Inside my tiny trailer, I dumped my worn uniform onto the floor. Exhausted by the suffocating environment, I wanted the cool comfort of my sheets and a moment of solitude. I pulled my comforter over my head and shaded my eyes under the filter of its soft rose tint. I couldn't relax. The noise of jet engines vibrated the trailer's thin walls.

Earlier that day the radar equipment in the air control tower had gone down. Without navigational assistance, I'd had to keep a motion picture inside my head: where the planes were, what they were doing, how close they were to me, to each other, their speeds, and what they wanted—to land, to touch and go, or to perform the acrobatic war dances of spiraling flameouts or sharp mid-air breaks.

Then an F-14 was in trouble: there was a helicopter exercise on the runway, and just to the right the Navy SEALS were training with closed-water explosives in the bay. The pilot's only way around them was to fly straight on runway heading and then make a hard-left turn at the upwind numbers. The fluttering helo on the left, the shards of water tearing into explosions on the right. As the F-14's air traffic controller I had to pray I didn't make a mistake. In the tower's Class Delta airspace the planes popped up out of nowhere like idea bubbles on a pictogram, all competing for my attention as they tried to make contact with the runway. There was no time to panic, no room for error. What would happen if the nearby explosions went wrong when the F-14 rushed by?

Controllers always took the blame somehow. The moment I spoke up I was instantly liable. While I stood watch over the airspace and the runways, someone else surveyed my recorded voice, listening and waiting for something to go wrong, to see if it was my fault.

I felt a knee sink into the soft give of my old mattress. The comforter and sheets jerked away, leaving me exposed in my black bra and pink underwear.

Adam Goodman*, a Navy SEAL, stood over me. "Damn, you look good! I should have done this a long time ago."

I reached down to pull back the covers. I curled my fingers around the sheet's edge and held it up to my chin. What was this guy doing in my room? I hardly knew him. I sunk down into the canoe-shaped mattress, folding inward. He straddled himself onto the bed. He separated my legs with his. I kicked up and down his shins. Our legs chafed against each other like two hands rubbing themselves for warmth. His rust-blonde mustache held the smell of the Corona he'd placed, teetering, on top of my alarm clock. Our hands braced against each other, fingers intertwined. He pushed down on me, I pushed up against him. I said nothing.

Goodman's eyes rapidly shifted left to right, searching mine, I assumed, for the cornea dilation that signals surrender. My right elbow shook, crumpled, and then he lay on top of me. He shifted the blankets away from my body. This was a Navy SEAL: trained to kill.

I had to think of how to get away, how to maneuver without upsetting him. As he plunged forward I slid to the left. I forced a small tentative smile *(Keep everything cool, don't upset him! Do not throw up)*. I had to make this whole encounter seem like harmless fun. I inched toward the edge of the bed, gathering the tossed blankets in an effort to conceal myself. But he rushed towards me fast. I brought my knees toward my chin.

"I didn't know you had a tattoo," he said.

Why would you? "Yeah, I got it when I was 18. I was going through a rough time, and—"

He wasn't interested. Again, he moved on top of me. Quietly, we worked our muscles against each other, skin rubbing, breath colliding. Legs kicking arms, thumbs, pressure points, skin and nails. The mattress struggled against the bed frame.

I breathed, measured his movements, watched his thrusts into the air, and found an opening. He relaxed his grip on me. Slowly, casually, I headed not for the door but for the clothes behind it. He sat, watching. I had to convince him.

"I was going to go out," I told him. My change of subject and the certainty in my voice seemed to have penetrated his anger.

He watched me, clearly judging the distance between me and the door, calculating my moves. Before I could zip my jeans, he stood behind me and wrapped his arms around mine. We wrestled for position, thrusting our hands at the air in front of us, striking out for either freedom or restraint. I hated myself. I hated the expensive apple-scented conditioner that masked the cold electric sweat steaming from my scalp as I fought him off. Bottles of perfume smashed over the tile. I felt myself give up.

Goodman moved me easily to the overstuffed reading chair, his knee pinning me in place. His right arm secured my shoulder, neck, and chin. I tasted my throat, trapped by a crusty yellowing elbow staring back at me. My bleary eyes watched him fumble with my CD player. With his left hand he inserted The Cure. *Show a trick/to make her scream/and then she'll run away . . .*

I am going to be raped, I thought, I am going to be raped and I cannot fight him off. The room spun counterclockwise. The mattress leaned on the dirty floor. His muddy tracks streaked and stained the room. The Cure spun louder. I followed the spinning around the room, kept it moving until the shadows in the periphery became dark. Drowning, faster and faster, I pushed everything deep into the vortex of my mind, down into the inner cold, distant core. Autopilot. I'd practice the flameout maneuver used for engine failure. No one would see the wings slicing inward, the power aborted in a desperate attempt to sustain impact. No one was there but us, plummeting out of control.

I leaned up, swallowed, and willed myself to do what I had to with my mouth—salt, sweat, skin, hair—I kissed him on the neck. He looked at me, shocked.

I will tell him what he wants to hear to get him out of my room.

"If you want," I said, "I'll go with you to your place."

"Really? Lt. Pierce wanted me to get two girls."

What? "Yes."

"You promise?"

"Yes."

"You do?"

"I do!"

He left the room in a run and I rushed to the door, turning the gold metal tab with my thumb and index finger and then shaking the knob to ensure it was locked. In vertigo, my mind saw the room as its reflection in the brass doorknob. I couldn't tell if the spinning came from me or the room itself. I couldn't decide whether to put on more clothes. I felt disgusting. Dirty, used, guilty. I could still smell his breath, the dirt on his hands, the stench of that putrid elbow, the air musty with struggle. I got into the shower and turned the water on as hot as it would go. The drops like bullets blurring my sight, scorching my scalp, filling my lungs.

In boot camp, the Recruit Division Commanders had warned us that complaining about individual discomfort during the gas chamber drill would disrupt the entire group. "You can say something if you want," they yelled, "but we will have to stop everything and start the whole operation all over again. So, you can take the option of raising your hand for 'training time out' bullshit, and interrupt everyone around you. We all have to go through this, so do it. Get it over with. If you leave before the event is complete, *we will* start all over again. Do you understand!"

"Yes, Petty Officer!"

I stood in the back row, squeezed in as an extra. My mask didn't fit. I had alerted them to this, but they only offered one size. Gas poured into the chamber. A thin veil of yellow haze like a polluted mist of spring pollen. At my side, Seaman Recruit James whispered *are you okay* through the plastic barrier. I shook my head.

"Raise your hand!" he said. "You're not supposed to breathe it yet. It's not fair, your mask doesn't fit."

I pointed toward the front and then toward my temple. James

understood and pulled my face toward his body, trying to block out what he could. Still, I was left unprotected. My fingers fit easily under the mask as I scratched my face and neck, both burning with the chemical stench of fuel digesting through my pores. The necks and hands of the others were red from the exposure. My eyes wept hot tears, stinging my cheeks like boiling water poured over a sunburn.

When our row was up, I was ordered to remove my mask, but doing so made no difference since it had never protected me. The discomfort everyone dreaded had already been my experience for 20 minutes. I needed to throw up. I tasted my throat, seared and swollen from swallowing poison like bleach. I focused on the pounding just outside. Feet smashing themselves into the greasy pavement to a familiar tune. I didn't hear the commanders shouting questions. *What is your name? Can you hear us? Look at her! Get her out of here! Do Not Throw Up, get outside!* Step, step, step, the cadence sang, "One and a two and a three and a four." Bang! Bang! Bang!—

Goodman had returned, punching at my door.

I sank against the shower wall and watched the water swirling around my feet into the drain. My back and neck raw, my head between my knees. One and a two and a three and a four, I watched my foot tap the water. Finally, the banging stopped. I looked into the haze, turned off the shower, and found my way to my clothes. I couldn't feel myself pull the jeans over my legs, the cream-colored sweater over my chest. Standing, staring, spinning, I let the vortex take over.

Bang! Bang! Bang!

"Christy? Christy it's me. Let me in!"

"April?" I asked through the keyhole.

"Yes! Hurry!"

I let her in, nearly shutting in her shirt as I locked the door. April's eyes traced the room's upheaval as she told me that Goodman had woken nearly everyone up by hollering her name though the rows of trailers and screaming that he needed to get laid. When April's roommate, Rachel, opened their door, Goodman shoved her to the floor and shook April awake, insisting that she join me and him.

The banging began again. We were both trapped in my room, Goodman pounding on the door. Since escape was impossible, we decided to fight him off together. We put our hands on the brass knob, squeezing each other's palms, and opened the door to Goodman's red face. The three of us fought in a blur of yelling and pushing. April pleaded for him to "Just *please* go away!"

Goodman's feet were locked into opposite corners of the doorframe. His fingers rooted themselves around the interior molding, while we strained our four hands and legs against his torso, hips, shoulders, thighs. April's fingers dug into Goodman's ribcage and I pushed against his legs with as much strength as I could muster so that he was bowed outside the doorway, holding on by his hands and feet.

Underneath his extended arms, I saw Sam, another airman, move from her trailer across mine toward the outdoor phone. Frozen, she mouthed, *do you want me to call the cops?*

Yes, yes! I nodded. I envisioned the police's arrival with lights, sirens. But the police didn't come. Not like that. Instead, after a long, long wait men appeared, positioned all over the gravel, some standing, some squatting, others further back, all with guns drawn.

Goodman smiled broadly at the sight of Turner, an MP who had failed to survive the Basic Underwater Demolition School. "What, is that your boyfriend? Is Little Rambo gonna save the day? Is he gonna beat me up? Look at those BUDS dropouts!" He took a casual sip of his beer. April and I rushed toward the pointed barrels.

The MPs buckled April and me in place and fled toward the station, where we were immediately separated.

I stared about the antiseptic holding room, counting holes in the perforated walls of the partitioned cell. Finally, the chief of police sauntered in, jerking my chair forward as he budged into the cramped space.

"Smoke?"

"Yeah."

"Were you raped?"

"No."

"No?"

"No!"

"Then why'd he leave your room?"

"I outsmarted him."

"You outsmarted him?"

"Yes."

"I find that hard to believe." Chief Strinberg licked tobacco flecks stationed at his lower lip. "All right. Tell you what. Your story and April's match up, and we just found Goodman, so—"

"Just found him?"

"Took two hours. He blew positive. He musta been pretty drunk before or kept on drinking. We found him closed in at BUDS' camp. Wouldn't come out."

Strinberg shook his cheeks. "Turner gave me a note he found last night. You wanna tell me about that?"

I told him Turner had given me a ride home from the Halloween party, but when we pulled into the lot across my trailer, the door to my room was open. Turner told me to remain in the vehicle. "I'd locked it before I went out that night," I said. "I know, because I had my key in my pocket. But Turner never showed me the note. He just said it was from Goodman, telling me to be careful or I'd be called a slut."

Strinberg laughed. "But you're not one?"

"No."

"You might want to borrow a jacket then."

"Why?"

"Honey," he leaned in. "You're wearin' a white shirt and a black bra."

The next day I piled into the duty van and let it point me toward the airfield. I shut out the conversations my co-workers tossed around the van, pressed my face against the cool windowpane and watched the tumbleweeds race the waves. Today NCIS was coming out to investigate, and I wasn't allowed to talk about it.

"I know who it is," Brittany hissed in my ear.

"What?"

"It was Goodman, wasn't it? He snuck into my room last night and said no matter what, I couldn't say he was there."

I looked at her, wide-eyed.

The officials from NCIS had the same questions Chief Strinberg asked the night before. Once they finished their interview, they left to snap pictures of my room. No one photographed me. Not the olive-purple bruises on my legs, or the uneven tears that ripped along my breasts toward the overdeveloped muscles in my back. The Mess Specialist that gave NCIS access to my room filled the whole island with the gossip. The only thing left for everyone to discuss was my guilt. Most people felt bad for Goodman.

Months went by, and rumors swirled. The first time I met my lawyer was one hour before the trial. "Do you understand the implications of your allegations?" she asked. We stood in an empty room within the Naval SEAL Headquarters, Imperial Beach, California. "It's too bad," she said into her notes, "Goody's going to lose his career. He just put on first class, too. The captain's going to bust him down."

I was moved like a wooden doll into the holding room with a large conference table set up for all of the witnesses, his and mine. People I rarely spoke to were going to testify: "impartial" witnesses meant to counteract the testimony of those who saw what happened.

"So, do you drink often?" Goodman's lawyer asked me.

"Sometimes."

"That's what you were doing that night?"

"What? No! I had just gotten off work."

"But you said in your statement that Goodman carried two beers in his hand."

"Yes."

"And you didn't drink one of them?"

"No."

"But you had beer in your refrigerator?"

"Two cans."

"To drink."

"To use on our hair!" I was surrounded. On my left was Master Chief Petty Officer Aroldo. The glare off his dress-white trident stabbed my eyes. My lawyer smiled dumbly at me, nodding her head. In front of me was the Commanding Officer, leaning over the podium. To my right was a wall of Navy SEALS. They were there as Goodman's peers: a silent, towering formation. Behind the wall of men was Goodman's father, a private investigator that had been following me—watching me, snapping pictures of me doing my laundry—for weeks. Standing directly beside me was Goodman.

"Petty Officer Goodman, what were you doing at her room?"

"I just went there to see if she wanted to go to the club—"

"That's not true!" I shouted, pointing my finger up at the Commanding Officer.

"SIR!" Master Chief Aroldo said, his stale coffee breath at my face.

"You say Sir, you understand me?"

My lawyer nodded.

I was asked why I didn't call out to anyone. Where was my room-mate, and why I didn't use the window? When I said I didn't have a room-mate or a phone, feet shuffled. When I explained that Goodman was outside, so getting out would only put myself right back into his hands, they considered. When I defended not yelling, they bristled. One of the officers smirked. "Do you not know how to yell?"

"I wanna hear you scream!" Petty Officer Sampson said on the second day of basic training. "I know you're not here to make Daddy proud! I know you are not here to find a damn man! I know that you have been beaten, hurt, abused! Why else do girls join the military? That's why you have to yell. None of this bullshit flowery voice. I won't have it! The next person that has the watch better not give some half-assed attempt at telling me what I need to hear when I walk through that door. Whoever has the next watch, do it right or be set back a week!"

Three years earlier, as a military wife, I learned never to yell. Even when my ex-husband tossed my body around the living room by my waist-long hair. I learned that the cops did nothing, that the military cov-ered it up, that I would be blamed for hurting his career.

It was our second day of boot camp, and I hadn't memorized the words we were supposed to call out whenever anyone who outranked us came to the door. I felt symptoms of stage fright: pounding headache, clammy hands, racing pulse. I'd thought if I moved away from my abusive family I would never have to yell again. I practiced in my head . . . *good morning! . . . good morning Petty Officer!* I was going to yell louder than I ever had in my life. I figured it was better to get dropped for screaming than be set back for not raising my voice. When the knock came, I knew before looking that it was her, Petty Officer Sampson. I summoned all of the frustration I had harbored for years and in a guttural blow yelled, "Good Morning Petty Officer! Airman Recruit Clothier, Division 265, Standing by for further instruction!"

Sampson shook her head in disbelief, "That was outstanding!" And it was. It was the first time I had heard my voice sound strong.

Goodman lost his rank and was awarded a dishonorable discharge. I lost my appeal for counseling. My LPO told me I had missed enough time. "Quit bitching," he said, "and get back to work."

Today Goodman is free, and I am walled in by windows, trapped into a service I cannot be released from: my time hasn't yet been served and we are at war. This is no time for silence. This is what I am trained for. After surviving hand-to-hand combat with a Navy SEAL, I recognize that while Goodman and I were in our separate worlds, neither of us knew how to make peace.

When a pilot calls to me in my control tower, I am charged to say something. I stand, phones ring, people scream, radios buzz. Outside I hear the deep rumble of an engine readying itself. A pilot corners the runway, listening for my voice.

*For the author's safety, this name has been changed.

ELIZABETH KEOUGH MCDONALD

Yes, Sir!

"…there's a sickness
worse than the risk of death and that's
forgetting what we should never forget."
— Mary Oliver, from "Tecumseh," *American Primitive*

I sit quietly as you demonstrate
to this heartbroken airman,
father of a one-month-old child,
his soldier-wife sent to Iraq, how he
must miss fucking. You poke your middle
finger through the bottom of a Styrofoam
coffee cup and rub it quickly up and down.
After all you are the senior officer.
The only woman in this group, I simply
look away and meet the airman in the eye.
I know he wants to cry, so I roll my eyes
upward as if this game is so-so boring.
I save him, but a piece of me drowns.

Yes, Sir!

When you call me into your office, the Chief
Nurse also present, to address why I would
think I need training in a field I have never
worked, you become angry and throw your
heavy pen at the table with enough
force for it to ricochet off my chest. I flinch in
pain. The black ink stains my shirt. The Chief

Nurse says, *That is enough* and asks me to leave.
Another military woman saves her man.

Yes, Sir!

Soon after, I am not promoted. I am unsure if this
is related to the pen or the complaint that me and
three nurses filed on you, the senior officer, who
thought groping us would better acquaint you
with the female troops. When you moved up from
Captain to Major, three of us left the military
and a fourth was sent to glacial Alaska.
Penance, a friend of cold places.

Yes, Sir!

My soon to be ex-husband,
a military man, calls me when he hears
my unit is mobilizing for war.
This is so exciting, he tells me.
His words become another
pen, a Styrofoam cup, a stray hand
to my breast.

Yes, Sir!

BOBBI DYKEMA KATSANIS

Bringing the War Home

first inhalation
steel-sharp with fear,
born into strangeness,
love that stings like fire.

a father:
big-bellied, deep-voiced,
cruel mouth of gold-capped teeth,
boot heel clicks on hardwood floors
like sight adjustments on an M-16.

held in his lap,
age seven,
teased so mercilessly
I summoned all the force of childhood
protest: urine, tears, and vomit.

framed in that house
are stories, secret, sealed
behind six pairs of lips,
beneath a gathering swarm,
whispers of new souls
schooled in misery,
fresh plums in tender flesh.

children growing a wolf behind their eyes
ready to snap,
with snarls and swaggers just like his,
piercing new lungs
with terror's metal scent.

can hope,
locked thirty years
in creaking echoes,
breathing, barely,
find its rusty key,
taste free, wide sky?

ELIZABETH KEOUGH MCDONALD

Every Night Is Footsteps

The Other Woman
says *it can't be scary,*
because he only grabbed her,
stalked her, didn't rape her.
Didn't do anything more.

Her friend says *his grabs*
were violent and painful
the way he followed her,
unseen, in the dark, came
from behind and did it again
and again. So now every night
is footsteps.

The military promoted him.
He was such an outgoing
sort—a family man, Christian and
a team player. They decided the
three female officers who
complained about him were
simply, like their friend, "a bad lot."
Like overripe tomatoes in the garden,
who would bother with them?

One by one, her friend says, *we*
were denied promotion, split up
from the others by different shifts
and assignments. One sent to Alaska
and three left the military. A husband

wanted to kick his ass. Another said
he would kill him slowly.

The Other Woman says,
*Goddamn. That bothered
you guys? That was nothing.*

VI.

GI JANE

Traditionally a derogatory name for military women, in recent years reclaimed to some extent as a positive term. See also: Queen for a Year, Wasted Money, Whatta Mistake, Winnie the WAC

DHANA-MARIE BRANTON

American Music

The mornings began with music. Piped in from the white Command Building, the music told the base to pause for morning colors. The sailors and Marines of Marine Corps Air Station, Iwakuni gathered in clumps on Japan's largest air base. We froze outside the grunt huts and on either side of the strip hangars, formed lines on the edges of detachment units and in the back of the base police station. Civilians toed the line, too. Military wives and Japanese civil servants stopped their cars. Dependent children stood solemnly in classrooms. Officers and enlisted were equal: eyes forward, arms glued, back a rod, mind on the red, white and blue. If birds sang, we didn't hear them.

Our home away from home looked like a model of regional American charm. Except for the bonsai trees peppering the landscape, the base felt like middle America. The main shopping square, a stone's throw from the Base Command Building, was an open-air plaza filled with pine benches, old-fashioned streetlights and bright red phone booths. Circling the plaza were low, modern buildings that housed the Marine Corps Exchange, a grocery store, cleaners, beauty and barbershops, a Wendy's fast food restaurant, and a 24-hour cab stand. Great care had been taken to give the base the look and feel of Smalltown, USA.

But the first day of my arrival I knew I wasn't in Kansas. I checked in at the military police station and was greeted by two Black middle-aged Marines.

"You must be Seaman Branton," the first said as I approached the counter.

Military rank is visible on one's sleeve, but his eyes were on a clipboard.

"Orders for Branton, DM, courtesy of Chicago, Illinois and the United States Navy," he read. "Completed boot camp at NTC Orlando, Florida and

Religious Programs Specialist A-School at Naval Construction Base Gulfport, Mississippi. Rate of RP, rank of E-3. Going to work for the Command Chaplain. *Seven-teen.*"

He'd miscalculated; I'd turned 18 a few weeks before, a day when I'd felt in charge of my destiny. But now, standing before a pair who reminded me of my father's drinking buddies back home, my palms were sweating and my face was hot.

A genial-looking older man emerged from a back office. If not for his flat stomach and regulation hair, he looked as if he could tape on a white beard and launch a side gig playing Santa Claus. His profusion of stripes— Gunnery Sergeant— made him the top banana of the Corps' enlisted heap.

"Welcome aboard, Ma'am. What can we do you for?"

His eyes rolled over my face and lingered at my mouth. I didn't know it at the time, but at MCAS Iwakuni the ratio of men to women hovered around 200 to 1. The Marines manning the Command administration offices knew exactly how many female sailors and Marines were coming for unaccompanied tours. They knew the single from the married, the childless from the mothers. They remembered your name, rank and hometown. The day a new woman arrived on base, the news spread like fire.

I'd just come from a sweltering Seabee base in Gulfport, Mississippi, where I'd been sent after boot camp to train as an RP, or Religious Programs Specialist. My classmates were a merry, exhausting bunch who drank like fish, cursed like sailors and played musical beds with astonishing glee. They seemed intent on proving that Chaplain's Assistants weren't squares, and though in my memory their last names are fuzzy, their faces still appear: that wild, red-headed girl from parts South named Mary; Cindy, who had brown hair and blue eyes and was so sweet-natured I nicknamed her Lemon Drop. There was Michael, that Trinidadian boy from Harlem; and Frederick, a jolly white giant who was always clamping his big hand on your shoulder, saying, *Sometimes you just gotta say, what the fuck!*

I usually declined their invitation to close the enlisted club and would return to my room to battle the giant, flying waterbugs that sat on the gray walls. If I worked the key quietly and flicked the light fast, I'd catch them lounging on my bed like sunbathers on the sands of Florida.

Early one sticky morning, I turned over in bed and so many wings left my blanket that I thought it was raining.

Our instructor, RP1 Robertson, was a mercurial, lethargic man who dismissed my sniffling about the bugs *(they were here first)* and had been spotted in town having his own beer-soaked evenings. But that final morning of "A" School, we stood sober and wide-eyed while Petty Officer Robertson revealed our destinations in the fleet.

We were poor and working class kids from battered cities and nowhere towns who never thought we'd see the end of our living rooms, much less the places RP1 began to sputter out. He called our rate, rank and surname, paused to let us die a little, then gave up the command—*Naval Air Station, Naval Support Station,* with the most important part trailing behind. *Rota, Spain; Keflavik, Iceland; Lockerbie, Scotland* and *Diego Garcia,* which sounded South American, but was off the coast of Sri Lanka. I held my breath when he said *RPSN Branton.* I was surprised to hear *Marine Corps Air Station* and just plain confused by *Iwakuni.* But things became crystal clear when he said Japan. Lemon Drop had me by the neck and Crazy Mary led the room in yelling. Frederick uttered something more befitting a Chaplain's assistant: *Jesus Christ!*

I went to the club with my shipmates that night. We stuck out our butts and chests and jumped up and down on the dance floor, thrilled to be young, drunk and going somewhere Mad Stupid. We held a shots contest that left us staggering to our rooms, squealing the same two lines: I'm comin' to visit you/No, I'm comin' to visit *you!*

I lost touch with my "A" School classmates, but suspect they discovered that every place, no matter how exotic, has a way of becoming normal. Still, what passed for normal in Iwakuni was not business as usual for the enlisted men and women stationed there.

It wasn't just that the base was home to several thousand unaccompanied Marines; complicating matters was the absence of available civilian women. Stern local parents did not approve of American men and their less than honorable intentions and the rural town's proximity to Hirsohima demanded strict enforcement of base security.

Still, the Marines of MCAS Iwakuni displayed a decorum around women I have not found since. Doors were opened, hats were tipped. Morning, noon and night you were greeted as Ma'am, and when speaking with you in uniform, they clasped their hands firmly at the front of their bodies or at the small of their backs as if to convey that they had disarmed their weapons.

Everything I know about men I learned in those first few months in Iwakuni: how the absence of women threw them off guard. If life in the States had them scanning women like flowers in a garden, Iwakuni made them notice the difference in every rose. Once, I saw a girl walk out of the chow hall and remove her hat to fluff her hair. A Marine exiting the hall stood for a moment, closed his eyes and waited for the fragrant cloud. It was as if the impromptu race for women forced men to slow down to take in your hair and the puzzle of your eyes. They checked out your body too, but not so much to critique its shape and heft. They seemed grateful your parts existed at all.

Enlisted men and women were housed in a series of four-story off-white buildings that fronted a long wall separating the base from a body of water. Far away on the other side of the water, a castle shimmered in the sun and moonlight. The castle and the seawall made the back of the barracks wildly romantic. Down below, the water slammed into sexy rocks and the mist jumped up to kiss your face.

I was leaving the seawall once in my first few weeks there, when I saw a Marine drop a pair of bright green ladies' shoes from the window of his third floor room to a woman standing on the ground below. They were laughing. At night I would hear exit doors at the end of each hallway creak open, and then the pitter patter of women's feet down the outside stairs.

Women snuck on the male floors, but men never came to ours except for Friday morning when the duty inspection officer white gloved every room in the barracks. That made the fourth floor a man-free zone, and fostered an atmosphere that felt more like a sorority house than a military barracks. Girls walked down the halls half naked, you could get anything by knocking on anybody's door and there was precious little pettiness and bitching.

Life might not have been natural by American standards, but there was something untamed and beautiful about the military women there. I was stunned by the way they carried themselves. No matter what they did on the second and third floors, in love motels out in town and in cars under the Iwakuni Bridge, they were some of the proudest, strongest women I've ever met.

I can still hear the gravelly laugh of Sargeant Sydney Harrington of Washington DC, see chocolate-colored Michelle who was in the Navy and wore a weave when it was still taboo. She had one of those eyes that wandered while the other one stood still, but she compensated for it with a perfectly high and round ass. Shannon Walters was a blond corpsman from Austin, Texas and Ana Marquez came from a close Cuban family in the Florida Keys.

There were formal friendships to be made on the fourth floor as well as informal lessons dispensed to newer girls from wisened girl-floor veterans, like the best way to sneak on the male floors, which grunt hut you wanted to stay away from when invited to one of their leatherneck mojo parties, which men only dated Japanese girls and which were rumored to be gay.

A good source of information was Lori Antonucci, a Corpsman who practiced Pilates before the world even knew what it was. You could find her laid out on the floor of her room, legs askance.

I once knocked to fire a name at her.

"Gay," she said.

"But he's married."

"Gay."

"He's got a wife and kids back in the States!"

"Gay gay gay gay gay."

I told her I'd seen him while I was setting up the Pentecostal worship at Marine Memorial Chapel. He'd been born again.

"You'd get born again too, if you was a gay Marine."

If the male Marines disapproved of gay men, they seemed to accept lesbians among their ranks as de rigeur. The Corps had been the last branch to admit women, and though it was 1984 they still hadn't gotten used to it. They distinguished between men and women the way some people do between students and coeds. Marines were male. Females who happened to be enlisted in the Marine Corps were called WM's. When men were griping and moaning about the place of women amongst the Few and the Proud, their female counterparts became *Whatta Mistake* or *Wasted Money*.

Willie & Mike was another moniker, one they must have used when discussing Sharon and Peg, two women who lived across the hall from me. We were billeted three to a room, which meant there were three beds, three hutches and three deep closets with their own individual lock. There was one shower/tub in each room, a single sink with a mirror and a set of long windows that, in my case, faced out to the seawall and the castle gleaming in the distance.

I didn't notice anything odd at first, until I realized that although people rotated and arrived, no one ever moved in with Sharon and Peg. They were solidly built white girls with thick heads of hair who went everywhere together. They walked to breakfast and ate eggs, then met for lunch and generally disappeared for dinner. I was always ready for catcalls or ridicule from the male Marines, but these guys acted as if Peg and Sharon weren't there.

I got my ear filled about the dangers of falling in love in Iwakuni during a brief but intense friendship with Corporal Vida Chambers. She was Trouble, something I should have known the first time I saw her wearing her dress greens and leaving the office of the Command Executive Officer. A visit to his office usually meant your ass was grass. She rushed into the women's latrine and I instinctively followed.

I found Chambers bent over a sink, breathing heavily, bathing her face in scoops of government water. I pretended to fix my hair, then stood there, staring.

"Are you all right?"

She patted her face with the regulation Kraft towels then scanned my face in the spotless mirror. She rolled her eyes and leaned on the basin as if for support. I was about to step forward when she looked at the floor.

"You got some big ass feet," she said.

Her brown eyes were plaintive and serious. It must have been obvious I was not street-smart: here I was, a big, brown potato. She didn't giggle at me. She saw what I was. My feet are size twelve. They are wide and flat, a gift from my six-foot-five Mississippi-bred father who, before doctors began cutting away limbs burned black by gangrene and diabetes, wore a fourteen. I launched into a monologue, relaying all this information, y'know, like I do, and I remember her stare. Her lip tilted up and she listened to the whole spiel from this green girl from Chicago, chattering about giant-sized Indian-blooded aunts. She waited for me to finish, then walked to the door.

"Pretty face, though," she said.

Chambers was the kind of girl my mother had never let me play with. She'd had experiences I wanted to hear about, seen things I never would.

A Lance Corporal told me one day after Mass that Chambers was bad news. I asked him why.

He shrugged. "She's a man."

"You mean a *lesbian?*"

"I mean, a man. Just steer clear."

What he meant was that she gave some of the best head on base and charged men for the pleasure. He meant that she talked about what she did as supply and demand, and said the exchange of goods and services was the world's only profession.

This note is legal tender for all debts, public and private, Chambers would quip, just to hear me protest. Our conversations were like that, ducking and spinning around each other until one was exhausted and the other was back on top again. She'd look at me, scribbling notes to be recorded religiously for my journal, and say I was the biggest ho she'd ever met.

I think I fell in love with her. It wasn't romantic love, but a surge of devotion and loyalty. I loved everything about Chambers: the way she talked, the way she dipped everything in a dollop of yellow mustard at the edge of her plate, that she was from Baltimore. That for her, joining the Marines had been a last-ditch way to keep herself out of jail, unlike my reason: a way to get away from my mother. That the next time I saw her on base, she smiled and said, *Hey, Boots.*

But long before my fun times unearthing the Japanese nightlife with Chambers, I felt the eyes of hungry men. Young, hardbodied jarheads were everywhere, middle-aged and older ones, too, walking in rectangles on base and running in formation. Marines were not like sailors who got drunk in uniform and wore their hearts on their dungaree sleeves. They wore Marine Corps t-shirts when off duty and had the same crazy barber. They loved the Corps and adored each other.

Their respect and adoration for each other seemed to forge some unspoken agreement. When it came to Black women, the brothers were given first shot. The white men peeked, then looked away, but the black men waved and stopped me on the street. They joined me at meals in the mess hall, plopping down trays before I could protest. I saw dancing eyes. Naughty looks and smiles. I had so many of the same conversations it felt like one long interview. I remember the regional contingent, brothers from Chicago and Detroit, St. Louis and Gary, Indiana, who harped on our Midwestern commonality. They were followed by the Southerners: brown, sweet boys from Mississippi and Alabama whose bashful, insistent gaze told me I reminded them of their grandmothers and aunts.

The boys from the east coast grinned from a distance. They were watchers, as if they were still navigating the hard streets of New York, Baltimore and Philadelphia. But I was watching them, too. It was clear what they wanted. I decided they weren't going to get it.

Their faces float in front of me like steam. John of the easy grin and chipped tooth; Charles, who poured so much sugar in his coffee it made me feel sick. I see that white Marine, whose name and hometown I never knew. In my first days he took long, hard looks. They weren't friendly or hostile, just appraising. Around my second month there, I saw him at lunch in the enlisted club. He was eating his meal, but he kept looking at me. Finally, he walked toward my table. I flushed, mostly because my Mississippi-bred father would not approve of what this Marine was about to say to me. But as he walked by, fumbling with his hat, he said just loud enough for me to hear: "You're the color of good maple syrup."

It was a strange, white thing to say, but I suspect his comment was a kind of murmur to the landscape of himself; a realization that the lines drawn with paint back home were personal and portable here at Iwakuni.

I see the men who went around in pairs, Lance Corporals Jackson and Rogers, Frank and Frank--Guitterez and Owens. Two guys who spent so much time together I nicknamed them Itchy and Scratchy.

For those men and many others, sex was thought of as a human necessity. Getting laid could be a glass of water, akin to eating and sleeping. When you were hungry, you went to the mess hall. When tired, to your bunk in the barracks. If in between the mess hall and the barracks, you could get with a woman, that was one more need satisfied. And a year or two in Iwakuni made a lot of women feel the same way.

James Patterson was a Sergeant from the dark side of Boston with a wife and family in Cherry Point, North Carolina. He laid a case out as logically as any lawyer about why I should take a drive to sit under Kintai Bridge or go with him to a love motel.

"You're married," I said.

He shot a little grin to his wedding band, then went on about the dog and kids, too.

"But they ain't *here*."

He said it like that, pressing down on the "here." I see him munching on unbuttered white toast, spooning out a half grapefruit, plain cheese omelet and cup of black coffee. I teased him about always eating the same thing. He had burn marks on the side of his fingers that reminded me of my daddy. I told him he shouldn't smoke.

"I don't even know you," I said, when I finally realized bringing up the subject of his wife didn't seem to matter.

"What you mean, you don't know me? All these times we sat together?"

He was right. It was morning and there we were, sharing sunlight and scattered dishes.

"C'mon, girl," Patterson said, leaning back in his chair.

He said *girl* a lot, called me *girl*. Said *c'mon girl, what you up against girl?* It wasn't just that he wanted to sleep with me. It was that he seemed to believe that I—or any woman—was *obliged* to stand in for his wife.

I didn't have the sense to be angry, so I'd just laugh, like I did when Chambers told me she was making a small fortune that wasn't coming from Uncle Sam. I knew what she was talking about and I didn't like it. I'd tell her about the Lance Corporal who lived on the second floor. He was from Charlotte and the first time he looked at me a hundred things started jumping in my stomach. She knew what I was talking about and she didn't like it.

"Forget these losers. You need to take that to the bank."

I'd say I wasn't doing *that*. She would snort. I loved to hear her snort. Then she'd pull something out of her head, from the wide world.

"You think all them men back in the gold rush days found their mines then ran around giving pieces away? All these fool women running downstairs, giving it away for free."

I'd get defensive. Tell her some of those girls were in relationships.

"They in somebody's *room*," she'd say.

"Don't mean you can't fall in love."

"*That* is the worst thing you can do. Boots, don't nobody have *relationships* here. Their *relationships* back in the states."

Iwakuni would teach me that lesson the hard way, along with many others. That much of what we deny bears truth. That life, and the love that comes with it, is terribly simple but extremely complex—and that it's almost always both at the same time.

Years later, I can see myself clearly, sitting with Sergeant Patterson a few weeks before he returned to his family in the States. We never went on a date, but by then Antonucci had passed on the news: he was an exceptionally skilled lover. I was flirting like my life depended on it. I ate with him every chance I could, and when I'd study him under my eyelashes I was not thinking about his omelet.

When I think of Iwakuni now, how it created a space that, if only for our tour, forced what was real and true to the surface, those last meals with Patterson come streaming at me. And when he looks up from his plate to say *I love my wife,* I finally believe him.

RACHEL VIGIL

At Ease

I went my first year in the Army without touch,
handshake or hug
restructured into hushed eyes, a strong back
highly pressed
sleeve on sleeve
two fingertips reaching for one form.

He was Platoon Leader and I, Platoon Sergeant—
siamese twins
poker kings
born back to back, but
a last-minute reassignment
the narrow alley of possibility

Something soft inside pleaded to stay after
friends trickling to clubs
shy reasons for nearness
scenery out of focus but these four eyes
damming-in
high banks of boiled composure

He grabbed my hand and kissed me hard
the instant the last guest
                turned his back
gave rein to the ragged thrum beneath his skin

The strength for hoisting a 50 caliber
lifted me to him

sinews cinched my waist
months of restraint
whispering directly
into my mouth

DEBORAH FRIES

Alabama

Fresh out of medic school in Wichita Falls, stationed
in Montgomery, first day there I meet the man I'll marry.
He picks me up in his black MG, tells me about the ward—
its interesting chronics and dull convalescents, split
shifts and staph and the need to clean everything with
Isopropyl. Tells me where to get white uniforms and
nurse shoes, how to manage time with Valium and dex.
That, he says on the way to the base, *is kudzu.* Racist
Town's off limits right now. He's not used to Alabama
yet, stateside rank and rules, after being in Bien Hoa
where he'd keep a sterile field with one hand to suture,
eat pizza with the other. A talker, whose sergeant's
stripes are stapled on, not sewn. *They busted me again*
he laughs, down-shifting: a clue. Second day, I attend
his class on packing the dead: unwanted government
skills that I can use here in the states or abroad—
practical as performing a trache with a ballpoint pen or
handling an evisceration like a spilled purse. Skills
I don't use. It's the summer of '68 and I spend my time
in lesser service: days consoling the sick, nights listening
to Steppenwolf on a blanket along the flight line with
another medic, smoking something bought in Selma—
the dark around us so mysterious, bloodless and sweet—
the song on the car radio telling me to close my eyes,
look inside, let the sound take me away. Even closed,
I can see the allée of blue lights. We lie along them,
half undressed in the hot night, our splayed bodies
helping to outline the great long aisle that welcomes
the fighter jets, glows brighter with their deafening
arrivals—lines and lines of cool blue lanterns that pull
the planes home to land in Alabama. Then take us away.

HEATHER PAXTON

Sand, Sweat and Gunpowder

Hussein stood by himself that morning, lurking in the corner of the guard shack. I pulled the HUMVEE up to the designated parking spot, grabbed my M-16, and walked to the front gate. Before he said hello, he handed me a box wrapped in a cheap blue plastic bag. I stared at the bag, not quite sure what to do with it.

I shielded my eyes from the never-ending sun in the clear Iraqi sky. "What's this?"

"A present. Perfume. Women should smell like women, not men." On his face was a mischievous grin.

"You need to think of me as a soldier, not a woman," I said. This wasn't the first time he had given me a gift, and I was torn between feeling flattered and horrified. His crush on me only seemed to get worse as time went by. His two wives didn't approve, and neither did my commander.

Hussein was the local Sheik's first-born son, and a critical asset in catching insurgents and gunrunners in Diyala province. One day it would fall to him to run his tribe and keep his people safe. My job required that I transport him every day from the front gate to the operations center to meet with my superiors. This made my attempts to ignore him difficult.

"I can't accept this, and you know it." I thrust the bag back into his hands.

The smirk on his face vanished, and he stared at me with his dark eyes. "Why? You not accept my gift because you a soldier, not a woman? Take it. You a woman too. You make me happy if take gift."

I snatched the bag from his outstretched hands. "Get in the vehicle." I barked. "We're running late."

After I dropped him off with my superiors, I stole away for a moment to my room. I untied the knot in the plastic bag and took out the box containing the perfume. Inside was a beautiful oblong glass bottle, a mixture of clear and smooth, milky and rough, like fine sandpaper. It was topped with a white cap shaped like a fresh budding blossom. A gold pendant hung from the neck of the bottle: *Parfum D'Or*.

The only scents I'd smelled for the past four months were sand, sweat, gunpowder and the overpowering cologne that our Iraqi interpreters poured on every day. I pressed the pump and a spray of perfume shot out, saturating the air around me. I savored its spicy bouquet. My heart ached for the world I left behind. I was tired of the stench of fear that clung to every pore of my body. I dreamed, just for a moment, that the fragrance of the perfume could bring me back home, back where I was safe. But no amount of perfume could cover my fear. So I put the bottle into my trunk, washed my face, and went back to work.

Two months later, Hussein was dead. Shot in the chest five times while driving home from work. The day I learned of his death, I took the perfume bottle out of my trunk. I pictured his mangled body on the side of the highway. I pulled the cap off and inhaled, trying to recapture the joy his present gave me, but it only deepened my grief. When he gave it to me, I'd felt normal, like a woman and not only a soldier. Its scent had brought me to my own home, away from bombs and guns and death. Inhaling now, I was sorry I'd never thanked him. He'd given me a sense of home, where I felt safe and where I was loved.

SHARON D. ALLEN

Iraqi Entomology

The only fauna we have around here are bugs and lizards and a snake or two. The bugs come in three kinds—really big, hugely scary cockroaches; really big, hugely scary camel spiders; and really big, hugely scary scorpions. And then we have these teensy beensy little gecko-lizard thingys. I have a theory as to why the lizards don't get very big around here. The cockroaches *eat* them.

I just saw a *huge* cockroach in my room. Naturally, I did what any combat veteran would do. I screamed my head off. Deb Charles, former Marine, jumped on the bed, and then screamed her head off. Melissa Mark was at the door, screaming. "Is it a *mouse?*"

I assured her it was not such an unscary thing as a teensy little mouse. It was a cockroach from hell. Mark, ignoring my urgent appeals for her safety, grabbed my boot and proceeded to beat the crap out of said cockroach.

But it wasn't dead. Oh, no. Its remaining two legs bravely dragged its nearly lifeless body under my bed.

"I think it's dead, now," said Mark.

"AAahhaahhhahhahahha!!" said Charles.

"You THINK it's dead?" said me.

Charles stopped screaming and offered that perhaps on our next day off we should clean the room. I agreed, saying we should move all the furniture toward the middle to sweep and mop and spray. And get some insulation to fill in the doorjambs and such. Then Mark said that perhaps we should get rid of all the food. Maybe that's what's attracting the mice and bugs.

"What food?" I said, innocently.

"Well, maybe like this Pop-Tart under your bed."

I dragged my duffel bags out from under my bed to ensure the complete totality of deadness of this roach. But it wasn't there.

"It isn't there," said Mark.

"AAAhahahaaaaahh!!" said Charles.

"It isn't there?" said me.

Mark grabbed the flashlight and searched for the roach. It wasn't dead. It wasn't even tired. She valiantly fought off the antennaed beast, with boot and spray. It was a fight to the death, and I think Mark's size tipped the scales in her favor. She outweighed her opponent, like, a billion to one.

VII.

MOXIE

Bold vigor, courage, fortitude and endurance.

DR. DONNA DEAN

Coming to the End of the VA Road

It'd be so easy, so much easier to do what they want, to give in. It could be done so cleanly and neatly.

It would feed the small living creatures, and maybe even the bigger predators, if they found me. If I did it well enough, my body need never be found. It's so hard on the hapless soul who finds a suicide.

They might think they won—another woman vet gives up.

But if I went up into the mountains, up to where the wolves are, and the snows, I'd be safe. It'd be so quiet and clean. So much of our blood has been lost, all for nothing. All that blood and death.

I could go up there and position my head so it would fall backwards. After one quick cut with the sharp, sharp straight razor, it would all drain out. Clean and red, shining and spreading on the snow, it would be useful as food while the snow lasted. In the spring it would nourish new growth.

ELIZABETH KEOUGH MCDONALD

To The Survivors

In the throes of a language I struggle
to understand, I hold my hands clasped
tightly on my lap, as if they would flap about
confused, or betray me.

Triggers, perpetrator, intrusive thoughts,
cognitive and *exposure groups,* the wretched
leftovers of *An Army Of One* and *A Few*
Good Men. Buckle up, buckaroo. My heart
the romp of a black steel toe boot.

As one of the female veterans in the
VA Women's Trauma Clinic, I learn
how to remember, so that I can forget.
I want to speak the tongue of my country:
the coded ache of what I carry.

Part of me wants to embrace the sorrows
that surround us. Shoulder for another woman
what burdens her. Part of me does not want
to know that any of us exist, because by giving
us a name, I call out to myself. The hole wider
than what I have closed.

ANNA OSINSKA KRAWCZUK

War Terrorism

We see statistics

not the flag draped caskets

we see statistics

not the mourner's faces

we see statistics

not the pain of sorrow

we see statistics—

fallen heroines and heroes—

sacrifice.

MARTHA N. STANTON

Prayer from A Prisoner of War

Time transpires unevenly
once in a while it paces
without anguish
without knowing.

"Miserere mei, Deus . . ."

Beauty forms
in moments of remembering
the intensity of your being.

"Conserva me, Domine . . ."

Awake or asleep
the subterranean ebb
of Your love
presumes
continuity.

"Vide humilitatem . . ."

MARTHA N. STANTON

Vietnam: The Sentry

Always before the sudden rain
Before the rustle in the tall grass
Even before the leaves move or shadows change
The cricket sings and sings.

But when the wind comes up
And the sounds of the grass are strange
And the leaves on banana trees are quivering plumes,
When the boom of war shudders the earth,
He stops.

Be comforted—
When all around are dead
When the stillness returns
When alone with the heavy
Humid stench of indifferent marsh
The cricket sings—
"You are not alone, I am still here."

DR. DONNA DEAN

Memorial Day Pow Wow

I smell it as I walk in
it's like coming home
sweetgrass, sage and cedar
 swirling out the door

blessing me.

The drum pounds
the singers exalt.
I don't know the words
they hit my soul

enter my heart.

Fancy dancers, traditionals,
grass dancers, jingles
and shawls
men, women and children,

trace the Sacred Circle.

The drum pounds
and the soft susurration of moccasins
keeps time.
I've heard the sounds forever
 they're always fresh

enfolding me.

A baby in a tiny buckskin

loincloth
on his daddy's beaded shoulder
smiles at the Elder
dancing next to him

he's safe.

Everywhere the scent of sweetgrass,
sage and cedar all around
it's in our hair and buckskins
it's in our Wal Mart clothes

cleansing us.

It's time for the veteran's Honor Dance
Indians always honor us
I'll get up and dance this one
'cause Indians really care

Indians remember.

After, some veterans speak
and talk about their war
Korea, Vietnam, no WWII this time
I decide that I'll say something

for women vets, you know.

I want to tell them of OUR war
about women vets
I walk to the center of the Circle
just a few words to tell them. I want

I want to tell them

but I can't, I just stand crying
unable to speak. Again.

Still, they give me honor
and thank me and welcome

me home.

So I sit back down and listen
to the drum
and tell myself that next time
the sweetgrass, sage and cedar

will help me speak, at last.

BOBBI DYKEMA KATSANIS

Listening for Poems

For everything that can be named, can speak:
the dead can speak, and animals,
heron, wisteria, and bell,
rock wall and ivy,
temple and the grave.
Love speaks, and so does mystery,
the redwood falling in the solitary forest
cries out, the bullet-wound
whispers in blood, the concertina wire
atop the fence swaggers and threatens.

Angels speak, and daylilies, and pears.
The serpent makes suggestions,
camels call, the desert vastness beckons.

The ice of winter tells its somber story,
everything with wings speaks up, sings out, ensorcels—
poetry is everywhere, like smooth stones on a beach.

Contributor Profiles

SHARON D. ALLEN

Combat Musician, Lost in Translation, Iraqi Entomology, and
New Definition of Dirt

Allen joined the Ohio National Guard in 2000, at age 22. She was deployed to Iraq in 2004 and left the service in 2008. She worked primarily as a petroleum supply specialist, then as a wheeled vehicle mechanic and heavy equipment operator, building and improving Forward Operating Bases for the American and Iraqi militaries.

Allen's writing has appeared in *Washington Post, Pittsburgh Post Gazette, Cincinnati Enquirer,* and *Operation Homecoming: Iraq, Afghanistan and the Home Front, in the Words of U.S. Troops and their Families.*

Allen's younger brother Luke was in the military, as was her grandfather, who was wounded in World War II and captured by the Germans. She is glad she joined the military and glad she went to Iraq, but doesn't want to go back. "I just wanted to do my part," she says, "and I did." In the Guard, she drove nineteen-ton trucks filled with diesel. Before she was mobilized to the Middle East, she concluded that being in a large vehicle with the word FLAMMABLE written on the side "in eighty-million point font size" might not be such a great idea. While deployed, she wrote numerous short, nonfiction accounts based on people she met during her tour of duty.

"Being in the military gave me a confidence unrivaled by civilian training," Allen says. "If my car breaks down seven miles from the next exit, I know I'll be OK, because I've road marched three times as far with a ruck on my back. The military taught me I can survive and thrive. It instills teamwork and leadership, and gave me a better perspective on the world. It provided me with a never-ending brotherhood of those who have gone before and those who will come after."

CAMERON BEATTIE
Leaping to Earth

As a freshman at Loyola College, Cameron Beattie joined the ROTC, receiving a scholarship to cover the remainder of her undergraduate education. The following year, she was selected to attend Airborne School. She graduates in 2009.

Beattie spent her childhood observing the military life. Her father, a Special Forces officer, was away from the family for long deployments, but she didn't understand what it was like for him until she lived part of it herself. In part, she sees ROTC and her future military career as a path toward finding her way into a life she watched for 18 years.

"Airborne School helped me build confidence," Beattie says. "I realized if I could jump out of a plane, I could accomplish anything."

JUDITH K. BOYD
The Joust

Boyd joined the Army in 1991, at 20 years old. She has served in Germany, Bosnia, Atlanta, Korea, Augusta, and Kuwait. After graduation from college she deferred entry into active duty to pursue a law degree, and then in 1996 began her Army career as a military intelligence officer. She transferred from military intelligence to the Judge Advocate General Corps in 1999 and spent the next five years as an Army lawyer. She left active duty in 2004 and continues to serve in the Army Reserves.

Boyd says she knew it was time to leave active duty when she was in Kuwait, waiting to see if the US would go to war with Iraq. As she watched the news of the UN arms inspectors and listened to US rhetoric, she decided that as soon as she could she would seek a government job that would provide opportunities to help shape policy rather than only execute it. In 2004 she went to work for the Department of Homeland Security.

During the last few hours of the first Gulf War, Saddam Hussein launched a Scud at the base where I was stationed in Kuwait," Boyd says. "The Patriot missiles—which had a history of unreliable performance—missed and the Scud hit the dining facility during mealtime, killing and injuring several soldiers. Several of the Scud missiles, if not intercepted by the improved Patriot missiles, would have definitely hit the buildings I worked and slept in. With a missile launched at me from miles away, there was nothing I could do to save my life. I was reduced to a position not unlike the ancient maiden for whom the warrior knights would fight a joust. The knight in black was Iraq and the hero in shining white, aptly named 'the Patriot,' was President Bush. My hero triumphed."

DHANA-MARIE BRANTON
Excerpt from *American Music,* a memoir

Dhana-Marie Branton joined the Navy's Delayed Entry Program when she was a junior in high school, at age 16. After boot camp she went to Religious Programs Specialist School at the Naval Base in Gulfport, Mississippi. She served two years in Iwakuni, Japan, then went to Point Loma in San Diego, where she ran the Base Chapel. Branton left the Navy and earned her BA at Loyola University of Chicago, and is now at work on her MFA at the University of Minnesota.

Branton left the south side of Chicago for boot camp in 1984, just before the crack epidemic decimated her neighborhood. She reports that many of her friends and schoolmates didn't survive those years.

"I don't think I'd be the writer I have become without my Navy experience," Brant says. "The four years in the Navy, particularly the two in Japan, let me uncoil from the stress that my life, family and culture had piled on. I became myself in Japan, rather than the person others expected me to be. I learned to own my self and my mind."

CHARLOTTE M. BROCK
Hymn

Charlotte Brock was commissioned as a Marine Corps officer at age 22. Two years later she was deployed to Camp Taquaddum, Iraq, with the First Force Service Support Group. She was a Communications Officer, responsible for ensuring that communications were set up and maintained on the camp. While at Camp Taqaddum, Brock met the Officer in Charge of the mortuary and volunteered to help him in his duties in her time off. Now 28, Brock has recently left active duty but plans to stay in the Reserves.

Brock's father is a Foreign Service Officer, so her family moved from country to country every few years. She has lived in Jamaica, South Korea, the Cape Verde Islands, Algeria, France, Mexico and Benin. One of her father's uncles, a Marine, died test piloting the Harrier; another, John Ripley, is a Vietnam War hero. She knew early on that she wanted to be a Marine. Although Charlotte's father initially thought she was too smart to go into the Marines, he is proud of his daughter's accomplishments.

"I have never regretted joining," Brock says. "I would do it again. But if you asked me that question at various times over the last six years, I would have given a different answer. I gave a lot to the Marine Corps; at times, I gave more than was reasonable and cared more than was productive. But the Marine Corps gave me at least as much: self-knowledge, incredible experiences, trials and tests and periods where endurance was the only way to make it through. Best of all, the Marine Corps gave me a circle of girlfriends that will last a lifetime."

CHRISTY L. CLOTHIER
The Controller

Christy L. Clothier enlisted in the Navy in 1997, when she was 20 years old, and was stationed at Naval Air Stations on San Clemente Island and Whidbey Island. She typically worked 8 to 16 hour days as an air control tower supervisor. At 26, she left the service.

Clothier joined the Navy to improve her life: steady pay, healthcare, money for college. While in the military she met the man she has since married, which she cites as one of her many positive experiences during those years. Ultimately, though, she realized she could not improve her life if she was putting it in danger.

"I left the Navy because I knew I would never feel safe or be able to protect myself from the people I was forced to work with," Clothier says. "I also did not support the Iraq war. The military demanded silent passivity. As a writer, I am rediscovering my voice, healing my wounds, and finding true freedom."

The author dedicates her essay to her writing teacher, Deborah Brown.

DR. DONNA DEAN
Coming to the End of the VA Road and *Memorial Day Pow Wow*

Donna Dean served in the Navy from 1963 to 1981. She was stationed in San Diego, Denver, Washington DC, Italy and Norfolk VA. She left the service at age 40, and after many years of treatment and persistent advocacy with the Veteran's Administration she is now adjudicated at one hundred percent permanent and total disability for Post-traumatic Stress Disorder. She is the author of two novels and many short stories, and a new work titled *Warriors Without Weapons: Women Veterans and PTSD,* due out in its second edition from MacFarland in 2009.

When Dean enlisted, the Vietnam War was heating up. She felt it was her duty to defend her country. Her father had served in the military, as had her grandfather and her (male) cousins: it was just something her family did. Dean saw military service as a way into a more interesting life, at a time when the only jobs open to her as a woman had no path for promotion and were "killingly boring."

"My PTSD is chronic and incurable," Dean says. "While in the Navy I was raped repeatedly and impregnated once, and went through a humiliating and degrading process to abort. I never had a good commanding officer, and endured denigration and open hostility throughout my active duty career. In this essay I put down what I was thinking and feeling at a very, very bad time, when what the VA was doing to me seemed to more than equal the horrors I experienced in the Navy.

My story does not have a happy ending. There's no point in lying about it. I can't honestly say the thoughts I wrote back then are no longer with me. One of the things they've figured out about PTSD is that it can cause substantive brain changes that impact cognitive functioning, memory and verbal fluidity. I'm very isolated and hard to get next to. I have to guard my back. I'm capable of going out to restaurants and movies, but I can't go to a concert or get on an elevator with a lot of people.

Thousands of veterans are coming back now from Iraq and Afghanistan with PTSD. The Bush administration waged war on vets, including me. Rather than beefing up the VA to care for these vets, they tried to take away PTSD as a diagnosis. Many of us are too sick to fight back."

BOBBI DYKEMA KATSANIS
Listening for Poems, Fort Dix, 1989, Bringing the War Home
and *Desert Storm*

Dykema Katsanis joined the 188th Army National Guard Band in 1988, when she was 17 years old. She served four years in North Dakota then transferred to the Minnesota 34th Infantry Division Band for her last two years of service. She played clarinet, piano and voice for events such as Officer Candidate School graduations, parades and goodwill tours. She was discharged in 1996.

Dykema Katsanis says she experienced benefits in the military she would not have wanted to do without: the Army paid for most of her undergraduate education, and in addition to the good musical experience she learned some valuable lessons, such as "working with and for people I couldn't stand." But the culture of the military, she says, is "anti-intellectual, sexist, and subliminally violent, and I have had to work hard to leave that all behind." She is currently a doctoral candidate at the Graduate Theological Union, Berkeley.

"I did not enjoy my service and nothing could make me want to re-enlist, Dykema Katsanis says. "But my experiences have made me more sympathetic to enlisted soldiers, especially those deployed in unjust and illegal wars on behalf of powerful people and well-heeled interests.

I am the sort of person who can enjoy looking out the window of a moving bus for hours. Many of the images in the poem 'Listening for Poems' traveled past the 'bus window' of my imagination, including the concertina wire, which I had to handle as part of a training on how to set up a POW camp. Looking out the window of the bus could serve as a good metaphor for my experience in the military: constantly trying to distance myself from an experience that I found trying to my spirit, and imaginatively living in a beautiful transitory world visible to but separate from myself."

DEBORAH FRIES
Alabama and *Hartsfield-Atlanta Baggage Claim*

Fries joined the US Air Force in the spring of 1968, during the Vietnam War. She was 19 when she joined, and after basic training and medic specialist training in Texas, she was assigned to Maxwell Air Force Base in Montgomery, Alabama. She joined to work in information services, but the wartime quota system made her a medic. She was honorably discharged at age 20, without serving her four-year enlistment. She left with her sergeant, a Vietnam vet, whom she married. She says that marriage and pregnancy seemed preferable to working in a field hospital in Southeast Asia.

Fries was the Poet Laureate of Montgomery County, Pennsylvania from 2006-2007. Her book, *Various Modes of Departure,* won the Kore Press First Book Award in 2004. She has poems in *North American Review, Cimarron Review, Terrain,* and other journals, including the premiere issue of *Cream City Review*. A recipient of a grant from the Leeway Foundation, she lives in Elkins Park, Pennsylvania. She received an MA in English from the University of Wisconsin.

When Fries joined the military, enlisted women were not being sent to Vietnam. By the time she left, they were. Employed for 15 years as a government public information officer, Fries says, "I have lived for a long time with the potential for being called up to perform civic duty in an emergency. I accept the duality of who I am—someone sustained by maternal, caring, creative and peaceful pursuits, yet still feeling a responsibility to be part of an incident response team if I'm needed. But I wouldn't join the military again.

"Decades would pass before I'd see old, grainy news footage from that era and realize that if I had it to do over, I would have marched for peace rather than for a base commander. I share the concern that men and women veterans of my generation feel when we watch our children voluntarily put themselves in harm's way."

VICTORIA A. HUDSON, LTC
Convoy Day and *Bosnia 1996*

Victoria A. Hudson joined the Army ROTC in 1979, at 20 years old, and was one of the first cadets to serve with an Army Reserve unit while enrolled in ROTC.

The majority of her service has been in the Army Reserves. With five mobilizations over thirty years of service, she has served as an officer in the Persian Gulf, Bosnia, and Iraq. She remains in the Reserves.

Hudson earned her MFA in 2008 from St. Mary's College. Her poetry, essays and short stories have appeared in *Milvia Street, Army Times, More Bridges, Ballyhoo Stories* and *Back Room Live*.

"Writing about my experiences is partly how I process information and integrate those experiences into memory," Hudson says. "I wrote 'Bosnia 1996' about a day I went on recon patrol with a couple of other officers to examine the remains of a blown-out bridge along the Sava River. A woman came up to me and motioned for my camera, which had a zoom lens. She looked through it, out over the river, and then passed it to an older woman, who passed it to a young man, who then passed it to an older man. When he was done he gave it back to the first woman, who again looked for several long moments across the river. When she handed the camera back to me, there were tears in her eyes. The older woman was crying, too. I looked through the lens, to the remains of the bridge span across the river. There were two men on the edge of the ruined bridge, jumping up and down and waving their arms. Without the lens they were just specks of color, but with it, you could make out their faces. The woman thanked me and returned to her family, where they all stood quietly, looking out across the water."

TERRY HURLEY
The Dead Iraqi Album

Hurley joined the Army in 1981, following her high school graduation. She has served in North Carolina, Georgia, Arizona, Virginia, Georgia, Kansas and at the Pentagon. Overseas, she has served tours in Germany and Korea, and deployed twice in Operations Desert Shield and Desert Storm, where she served in Saudi Arabia and Kuwait, as well as Operation Restore Hope in Somalia. She has worked primarily in communications, but also in Personnel and as an Equal Opportunity Officer.

Hurley left the service at age 40, on medical retirement. She would join again, if she could do so as an instructor or mentor to incoming servicemembers.

"My military experiences have made me the woman I am today," Hurley says. "As I write about these experiences, my life becomes clearer. I have changed. I am more focused. I see the world through opened eyes."

ANNA OSINSKA KRAWCZUK
War Terrorism

Krawczuk joined the Women's Army Corps in 1955 in Newark, New Jersey, at 18 years old. She'd only been in the US for five years when she became an American citizen, just prior to her deployment. She served overseas, mostly in Munich, after the American occupation of Germany was lifted. She worked in a clerical capacity; part of her job was to run the film projector for officer briefings, some of which detailed the aftermath of liberated concentration camps. She was honorably discharged at age 21.

Krawczuk was born in Warsaw, Poland, to Ukrainian parents. Her family escaped the 1939 German invasion, but her father died in 1940. Krawczuk, her mother and sisters ended up in a German labor camp. In order to be accepted for immigration to the United States, her mother worked as a live-in cook while her daughters lived in an orphanage. Eventually the family was reunited. At age 17 Krawczuk graduated from high school and wanted to go to college. One day, she passed a recruitment station in Newark, NJ and saw the sign advertising the GI Bill. Tearfully, her mother signed the enlistment papers.

"My experiences in the military changed my outlook on life, Krawczuk says. "I came to understand the real dedication, devotion and patriotism of American soldiers. For the first time in my life, I was exposed to the diversity of Americans, both women and men, from all corners of the USA. Military camaraderie is something you never forget.

I definitely would feel obligated to join again, especially after September 11, 2001. We need to have dedicated people to protect our freedom and country. But when this war started it became clear that the administration in DC did not want 'evidence' of casualties shown on TV—thus the blackout on TV news of their arrivals at Dover Air Force Base. They deserve better than to return home in flag-draped caskets for no one to see."

ELIZABETH KEOUGH MCDONALD
Yes, Sir!, To the Survivors and *Every Night is Footsteps*

"The military is not something I want to talk about—only write about in my poems, McDonald says. "I am not the wonderful person I was before being in the military and even as I write this I am filled with sadness."

McDonald lives in Gallup, N.M. She received the 2008 Artist-In-Residence award from the Aspen Guard Station, San Juan National Forest.

HEATHER PAXTON
Scent

Paxton joined the US Army Reserves in 1998, when she was 17 years old. She was called up for active duty and went to Iraq in 2003, where she worked as a Civil Affairs Specialist, helping local citizens restore their lives by rebuilding schools, hospitals and government buildings. She left in 2006.

Paxton's mother, who is also in the military, instilled upon her the need to serve her country in some way, whether through the military, volunteer service or government work. She would join the military again; she says it has made her who she is, and has given her a strength she would not have had otherwise.

"For a long time after I came back from Iraq, I was plagued with dreams and flashbacks," Paxton says. "My writing became my therapy, helping me to cope with the experiences that so troubled me. I am forever changed by what happened to me in Iraq, but whether it is for the better or worse has yet to be determined. My experiences differ from so many because I developed meaningful relationships with Iraqi citizens. I met their families, saw where they lived and saw how the war was affecting them. So often, we think only of the soldiers, but really I was over there fighting for their right to security and happiness, too."

KHADIJAH QUEEN
Stretcher I, Stretcher II and *35 x 36*

Queen joined the Navy in 1998, at the age of 22. After boot camp, she went to sonar technician apprenticeship school at the Fleet Anti-Submarine Warfare base in San Diego and in 1999 was stationed on board The USS Cole in Norfolk, VA.

Queen's work has appeared in numerous journals, including *Poemmemoirstory* and *new ohio review,* and has twice been nominated for the Pushcart Prize. Khadijah's first poetry collection, *Conduit* (Black Goat/Akashic Books), was published in 2008. A video/sound/performance artist, Cave Canem Fellow, and founding member of Red Thread Collective, she holds an MFA in creative writing from Antioch University Los Angeles. She is currently a graduate fellow in studio art at the University of South Florida.

Queen left the Navy because she knew that she was "an artist at heart, and the option to be that fully was not possible with continued service." She says she would not join now, but that she doesn't regret her service.

"I started on the road to becoming a writer during the last year and a half of my service—starting with a poetry course I took online," Queen says. "I think that in addition to helping with college costs, and therefore

enabling me to study literature and writing seriously, the military expanded my sense of myself—I learned I could accomplish what I set out to do,
no matter how difficult. Writing is a discipline. Spending time in the Navy
made discipline a greater part of my life, and as such helped prepare me
for a sustainable writing life.

I knew many of the survivors on board The USS Cole at the time of
the October 12, 2000 bombing. I knew two of the dead and most of the
injured. Three people in particular inspired these poems, and I felt that
the complexities surrounding the events made poetry a necessary reaction."

K.G. SCHNEIDER
Falling In

K.G. Schneider joined the Air Force in 1983, when she was 26 years old. She spent eight years in the service, stationed in Texas, Illinois, New Mexico, England, Germany and Korea. She began as a jet engine mechanic, and two years later she was commissioned as an officer. She spent her career on tactical fighter aircraft.

Schneider was not called into action for the first Gulf War; she volunteered to go. She wouldn't join up to serve in the Iraq war, but says she would go if she were still on active duty: she believes that service is often about obligation to your peers, not to the military.

"The essay published here is about language, in part, but it's also about what every soldier feels when she joins up," Schneider says. "I feel very grateful for the opportunity to have served in the armed forces and for the experiences I gained there. Writing is how I express my gratitude: so that they who served with me can be remembered."

MARTHA N. STANTON
Prayer from a Prisoner of War and *Vietnam: The Sentry*

Stanton commissioned in the Air Force in 1951, during the Korean War. She also served in Germany, England and Vietnam. In Vietnam, she worked as a Field Reporter, where she was responsible for covering the progress of the agreement between Presidents Nixon and Thieu known as Vietnamization. Stanton retired in 1971, at age 49.

"The assignment in Vietnam was the most intense of my US Air Force career," she says.

ELAINE LITTLE TUMAN
Edit and Spin

Tuman joined the Army in 1982, at 23 years old, as a Morse code interceptor, and also trained as a Russian linguist. She served as a broadcast journalist in the Army Reserves, where she was deployed to Guantanamo Bay, Cuba and to Sarajevo, Bosnia. As an Illinois National Guardsman she was deployed to Afghanistan in 2004-2005 as a military intelligence interrogator.

Tuman is a retired reservist at age 49. She wants to establish a full-time civilian career, and no longer wants to risk more deployments and time away from her family.

"My experiences have made me more determined to write and to create. I have more of an awareness that life is precious and short. I am more tenacious, and less embarrassed to be forthright with people.

I do not support a draft, but I do think that more people should consider joining the military," Tuman says. "Service is an important rite of passage, or used to be. If they don't support the current administration, perhaps they should join the military first and enter politics or public policy later. Their voice for change will be treated with more respect."

RACHEL VIGIL
Deployment, At Ease, Stay in Your Lane, Gear Up and *Commander in Chief*

Vigil joined the Army at age 25, in 1998. She studied Arabic at the Presidio Monterey Defense Language Institute, and was subsequently stationed in Texas, Arizona, Georgia and California. She served in Operation Bright Star in Egypt immediately after September 11, 2001. She worked as an Arabic linguist and voice interceptor for the Army Intelligence Corps.

Vigil has done MFA studies in Creative Writing and Poetics at Naropa University in Boulder, Colorado. Her work has been published in *War, Literature, & the Arts; The Common Review; Poem; Blue Line; The Inkwell; Combat; Copper Nickel* and many others. She received the Amy Gruneberger Memorial Poetry Award in 2005 and was a finalist in the Cleveland State University First Book Contest in 2006.

Vigil signed up under the condition that she would be able to study Arabic. She planned to leave the military in 2002 at the end of her four years, but Arabic linguists were stop-lossed after September 11, 2001 and her service was extended another two years. She reports that having security clearance changed her perspective on many things. She was a "card-carrying young Republican" when she entered the service, and an active Democrat when she left.

"I have no desire to serve the [Bush] administration's objectives, and nothing would talk me into joining again, not even as a contractor. I don't regret having served my country, injuries and all. I used to call it the best miserable time I ever had. Living in a functioning commune produces change in a person no matter who you are. There is a kind of dignity in hard dirty work and a shared closeness between the workers at the end of it. I love it when strangers help each other, and I saw that so much more often in the military than in the civilian sector.

I joined to learn Arabic, and that has been a growing experience as well. Studying the language and culture taught me a lot. So much is taken out of context or reported in the American news media without an understanding of basic language, geography, and culture. It's no wonder we don't understand each other. I saw a lot of misunderstanding. There were so few linguists and so many strange situations."

ACRONYM GLOSSARY

550-cord	lightweight nylon rope
AK-47	an assault rifle of Soviet design
BX	Base Exchange. A general merchandise store on a military base
BUDS	Basic Underwater Demolition School
C-130 (Hercules)	a four-engine turboprop cargo aircraft
DCU	Desert camouflage uniform
D9 dozer	a large tractor bulldozer
D7 dozer	a medium tractor bulldozer
E-3	Echelon 3, a military rank
F-14	a shipboard fighter aircraft
FUBAR	Fucked Up Beyond All Recognition
HMMWV	High-Mobility Multipurpose Wheeled Vehicle. Also known as a Humvee
IED	Improvised Explosive Device
LPO	Leading Petty Officer
M-16 A2	Military assault rifle
M4	Military assault rifle
MCAS	Marine Corps Air Station
MRE	Meals Ready to Eat (field rations)
MOPP suit	Mission Oriented Protective Posture gear, for protection against chemical and biological attack.
MP	Military Police

NCIS	Naval Criminal Investigative Service
NVG's	Night Vision Goggles
NTC	Naval Training Center
POW	Prisoner of War
PTSD	Post-traumatic Stress Disorder
PT suit	Army jogging suit
ROTC	Reserve Officer Training Corps
RP	Retained Personnel
RPSN	Religious Programs Specialist
SEAL	Navy Sea, Air and Land Forces. The Special Operations Forces of the US Navy
TI	Training Instructor
VA	United States Veteran's Administration
WAC	Women's Army Corps
WAF	Woman in the Air Force
WM's	Women Marines

LISA BOWDEN is an editor, poet and award-winning designer. As co-founder and Publisher of Kore Press, she has been a champion of women's writing and a literary activist. She has developed contemporary writing projects and curated lectures, readings, workshops, panels and site-specific, improvisational writing collaborations. Lisa is the editor of *Autumnal: A Collection of Contemporary Elegies* (audio, Kore Press, 2007).

SHANNON CAIN is the fiction editor for Kore Press. Her work has been awarded a Pushcart Prize, an O. Henry Prize, and a creative writing fellowship from the National Endowment for the Arts. A lifelong activist for peace and social justice, her first act of civil disobedience, at age 10, took place outside the Danbury State Prison, in solidarity with the Vietnam War protestors detained inside. She held a sign handmade by her mother that read "War is not Healthy for Children and Other Living Things."

HELEN BENEDICT, a professor of journalism at Columbia University, is the author of four novels and five books of nonfiction, many of which concern social justice and women. Her writings on women soldiers won the James Aronson Award For Social Justice Journalism in 2008, and her book, *The Lonely Soldier: The Private War of Women Serving in Iraq* will be published by Beacon Press in the spring of 2009.

KORE PRESS

As a community of literary activists devoted to bringing forth a diversity of voices through works that meet the highest artistic standards, Kore Press publishes women's writing that deepens awareness and advances progressive social change.

Kore Press has been celebrating the genius of women through publishing since 1993. Greek for *daughter* and another name for Persephone—the mythic figure whose re-emergence from the underworld marked the changing of seasons—the name *Kore* expresses our belief in the power of the creative process and the conviction that women can change the world.

To purchase books, make a tax-deductible donation to support the work of the Press, or for information on how to submit a manuscript, please visit us at www.korepress.org.

Why Kore Press publishes women

1. In the history of the National Book Awards, 29 percent of the winners have been women.

2. As of only a few years ago, women constituted 17% of the opinion writers at *The New York Times,* 10% at *The Washington Post,* 28% at *US News & World Report,* and 13% at both *Newsweek* and *Time.*

3. Of the 137 authors in the recent *Norton Anthology of American Literature,* less than one-third are women.

Kore Press acknowledges

TUCSON PIMA
ARTS
COUNCIL

Arizona
Commission
on the Arts

NATIONAL
ENDOWMENT
FOR THE ARTS

COLOPHON

Powder was designed and typeset in August and September in Tucson, Arizona. The text is set in the unadorned, modern face of Myriad Pro Light with Myriad Tilt and Sketch display types. Layout was done on a Mac PowerBook G4 in InDesign, with image-editing in Photoshop. A few photographs were scanned on an old Epson Stylus 2500 printer-scanner. Two years in the making, from first call for submissions to printing press in Michigan, this collection (or *garland,* from the Greek for *anthology*) has come to you from the strong hands and determined minds at Kore Press. Appreciation goes to the writers for their courage to create and tell the truth; to Deb and Christina for assistance; to Eve for her discriminating eye; to Karin for the title—from *Gunpowder* to *Powder;* to longstanding friends, family and supporters of Kore; and to Shannon for bringing the idea to the table.